SPANISH

LEARN 35 VERBS TO SPEAK BETTER SPANISH

by Peter and Helena Roberts

For all novice Spanish speakers visiting Spain
—or any other Spanish-speaking country.

An English-to-Spanish language book, following on from its companion book, "Learn 35 Words to Speak Spanish". This book teaches 35 selected useful verbs which will allow you to speak better and more fluent Spanish.

Happy Holidays in Spain

Other language books by Peter and Helena Roberts include their "Learn 35 Words to Speak..." series from Russet Publishing. Spanish, Italian, Portuguese, German, French, Greek, Welsh, and Irish-Gaelic.

Also, this "Learn 35 Verbs to Speak Better..." series from Russet Publishing. Spanish, French, Italian, and Portuguese.

First edition: 2021
Version 1.0

Published in the United Kingdom
by
Russet Publishing
russetpublishing.com

ISBN 978-1-910537-49-7 Electronic Version
ISBN 978-1-910537-48-0 Printed Version

Copyright © 2021 Peter and Helena Roberts

"Learn 35 words to speak" is the copyright trade phrase of Peter and Helena Roberts.

"Learn 35 verbs to speak" is the copyright trade phrase of Peter and Helena Roberts.

Your comments and corrections are welcome
peter.roberts@russetpublishing.com

SPANISH	1
THE ROBERTS LANGUAGE LEARNING SYSTEM	6
A WORD FROM THE AUTHORS	7
INTRODUCTION.	9
LEARN 35 VERBS TO SPEAK BETTER SPANISH	9
PRONUNCIATION—VERY IMPORTANT	10
WHY ONLY 35 WORDS AND 35 VERBS?	10
1 OUR OBJECTIVES.	**11**
WHAT YOU NEED TO KNOW	11
THERE ARE THREE KEY PARTS TO OUR OBJECTIVES.	11
LEARN THE PRONUNCIATION REALLY WELL	12
2 SPEAK THE 35 VERBS.	**15**
TO INFINITIVES AND BEYOND	15
THE 35 VERBS	16
THE PRIME VERB TABLE	19
3 SPEAK THE INFINITIVE.	**27**
TO ENJOY SPEAKING SPANISH	27
THE SEVENTEEN INFINITIVE EXAMPLES FROM THE PRIME VERB TABLE	27

4   SPEAK THE PAST TENSE. 41

I HAVE ENJOYED SPEAKING SPANISH 41

WHAT IS A TENSE? 41

THE PAST TENSE 41

FIVE 'MUST LEARN' PAST PARTICIPLES. (PPS) 45

5   SPEAK THE PRESENT TENSE. 53

I ENJOY SPEAKING SPANISH 53

THE PRESENT TENSE 53

'MUST LEARN' PRESENT TENSE WORDS. 54

HOW TO MAKE A STATEMENT NEGATIVE. 55

6   SPEAK THE FUTURE TENSE 71

I SHALL ENJOY SPEAKING SPANISH 71

THE FUTURE TENSE 71

SIMPLE FUTURE SENTENCE CONSTRUCTIONS 71

IMPLIED FUTURE CONSTRUCTIONS 73

7   YOU CAN SPEAK SPANISH. 79

YOUR DREAM COME TRUE 79

SOME THINGS YOU CAN SAY FROM OUR "LEARN 35 WORDS TO SPEAK SPANISH" BOOK. 82

SOME THINGS YOU CAN SAY FROM CHAPTERS 2 TO 6 IN THIS BOOK. 84

Some things you can say by adding in words from Chapter 8 of this book. 85

8   SOME USEFUL STUFF. 89

FOR YOU 89

A FEW FUTURE, PAST AND OTHER MISCELANEOUS WORDS AND PHRASES 89

CARDINAL NUMBERS 91

ORDINAL NUMBERS 92

MONTHS OF THE YEAR 93

DATES OF THE MONTH 94

DAYS OF THE WEEK 94

CURRENT YEARS 95

THE TIME 96

THE ROBERTS LANGUAGE LEARNING SYSTEM

The main objective of Peter Roberts' rapid language learning system is that people should learn a minimal *fluent* core of words and verbs so that they can, from the start, go out in a foreign country to speak confidently and express their needs without a phrase book in their hands.

If you can speak your requirements with confidence and with the correct pronunciation (which Peter and Helena's books teach for *every* word), you will be able to order a meal, coffee, tea, wine, beer, a hotel room, a hire car, a train or bus ticket, entrance to a museum or art gallery, and anything else that you can point to. What more do you want on a holiday? Not much.

And, of course, you are not interested in hearing a native speaker tell you his opinions on the recent elections, on the state of the country's economy, or on recent serious crimes; you get enough of that on the TV at home when you are not on holiday. The Roberts language system will not equip you for conducting an abstract conversation with a Spanish native speaker; frankly, even two years of book study will not do that for you.

So, the Roberts method doesn't give you anything you don't want; just what you do want. Which is ideal!

Unfortunately, there is no other way to learn this material but to sit down and study it for a week or ten days. Our suggestion is that you set aside a regular time each day with someone else—preferably your proposed travel partner—and learn and test each other until you are sure that you know all the initial 35 verb-words that I have selected in the Chapter 2 table below. And, until you can say their pronunciation correctly without thinking!

A WORD FROM THE AUTHORS

A few years ago, we worked on and published a series of books entitled, "Learn 35 Words to Speak…" The books in that series have been for sale on the Russet Publishing website as PDF electronic books, which help to fight global warming.

With this, our subsequent "Learn 35 Verbs" system, in your head, you won't need a clumsy phrase book!

Go to our website (russetpublishing.com) to see how electronic books can help to fight global warming: You can see all of our books there.

We prepared this booklet for holiday makers, choosing the 35 verbs that you will need. We have received a good feedback from people who have used our system. You can see some typical complimentary comments on the Russet Publishing website.

To let us know that you have enjoyed our book and that it was useful, please email us at peter.roberts@russetpublishing.com

Don't forget to learn the reduced number of initial verbs and tenses thoroughly *before* your holiday if you possibly can. On the other hand, perhaps it will while away the time at the airport on your way out, or under a sun umbrella on a hot beach where you can then order your glass of water or lemonade fluently.

Best wishes from Peter and Helena Roberts.

Professional Input. *The colloquial Spanish content of this booklet has been checked and approved by a professional translation firm using a native-speaking, qualified Spanish translator.*

Introduction.

LEARN 35 VERBS TO SPEAK BETTER SPANISH

Yes, really! If—on top of the 35 words from our earlier series "Learn 35 Words to Speak Spanish"—you learn the 35 verbs that this book contains, you will be able to speak more Spanish than you ever thought possible in a short time! Try it and see. It will work!

Let me say from the start, that when I say on the cover of our books, *"With only 5% of the usual time and effort",* I do not mean that for 5% of the effort you can get 100% of the language. No. What I mean is that we are providing 5% of the language, curated for your benefit, to provide the minimum knowledge that a beginner will need to start to speak Spanish so that you can increase the fun and enjoyment of your overseas holidays. As a beginner, you couldn't do this for yourself, so we have done it for you. That's all we mean.

Our '35 Words' books sell all over the world, helping people with their first steps towards speaking up to seven European languages.

You can use this book without having used our, "Learn 35 Words to Speak Spanish" book but you would be advised to spend a week studying that book first—it tells you how to ask for anything that you want. This book tells you how to explain to people that you have a need for something, to ask questions, and to inform people what you intend to do. So, please consider using the "35 Words" book first and this book second.

Pronunciation—Very Important

In every chapter, we provide an acceptable (home-spun) phonetic pronunciation for each word that we use. You are obliged to learn the pronunciation each time you use a new word. Because our books concern speaking and not reading and writing, they concentrate on your learning the words in their phonetic form. Frequently, the actual Spanish words are printed in grey to make them less prominent.

One of the most important aspect of pronunciation is the vocal emphasis needed on different parts of words. Our book underlines the emphasised part of every word, making the flow of your speaking sound familiar to a native speaker

Remember that **pronunciation is very important**. Look at the phonetic explanation for pronouncing each new word and practise each word faster and faster until it sounds like a single word and until you can automatically say it as a single word without having to think about it.

Why only 35 words and 35 verbs?

Because then you won't have to struggle with a phrase book when you want to speak! No waiter, bus conductor, or Spanish citizen is going to hang about while you struggle in a book to find the phrase you need, are they?

1 Our Objectives.

WHAT YOU NEED TO KNOW

Put in a nutshell, we have looked at the 55 typically-learned verbs in a recreational second language, including the 7 typically-learned tenses and the six verb-persons within each tense, and we have cut these down to 35 verbs, 3 tenses, and 1 verb-person. That is a reduction of 2,100 verb-phrases to 105 verb-phrases—which is a 95% reduction. A reduction of workload to 5% of the usual.

You would not be able to do this for yourselves, which is why you have bought our book. We have done it for you. It means that, in practical terms, you would only need to spend two to four weeks to fluently speak your holiday language instead of the usual two years. With our system, the light at the end of the tunnel comes much quicker.

This is not idle speculation when you consider that the 95% that you will not learn is material that you will never actually need and which you will, therefore, inevitably forget through lack of use.

There are three key parts to our objectives.

Firstly, you have learned only the 35 Words needed and now the 35 Verbs. **Do not become tempted to add to these words and**

verbs until you are absolutely fluent in speaking them. i.e. you can speak them without thinking.

Secondly, by all means, carry a small English-to-Spanish-to-English dictionary with you but **do not attempt to use it while talking to someone**. If you need something important, then look up the word in advance and learn it so that you can speak it without a book in your hand.

Thirdly, keep re-checking your **pronunciation** all the time. It is too easy to fall into bad pronunciation and emphasis habits and thus allow your ability to communicate to deteriorate.

Learn the pronunciation really well

Learn it from the start and don't let it slip. We teach the pronunciation of each word as you are introduced to it. That means you don't have to fathom out and learn any complicated rules; yet you will speak the words we teach, perfectly understandably.

For example, verb 31 in the table: the infinitive '**to believe**'.

31	**to believe**		Written: creer
	Pronounced: **cray-<u>air</u>** *[air pronounced as in bear or care]*		
	All infinitives emphasise the final vowel, as underlined.		
	Emphasise the vowel underlined - if any.		
or			
	Yes,	I	understand.
	See	**yo**	**en-tee-<u>en</u>-doh**
	Sí,	yo	entiendo

The 'doh' is half way between 'dough' and 'dog'.
Note that you must emphasise all underlined vowels.

You will notice that, although there is a word for 'I' in Spanish, which is 'Yo', they do not tend to use it in casual talk. Entiendo actually means 'I understand', but in the table, I have put the 'Yo' in front to emphasise that it is you yourself to whom you are referring and it is safer when you are a beginner.

Our system is designed so that you do not have to learn all the many rules for pronouncing Spanish, but as you go through this book, you will notice that there are a few rules that we follow:

Always emphasise the last syllable of any infinitive.

Normally emphasise the next-to-the last vowel of any word. If you are not certain about a word, then adopt this emphasis rule. In direct contradiction to English, the Spanish sound the letter 'r' in many words. For example, in English, we would say 'particulah' without pronouncing the r at the end of the word. If it were a Spanish word, they would say 'particular', sounding the letter r quite clearly. Americans tend to sound their letter 'r' in most words.

Whenever a word begins with the letter 'h' it is silent.

When the letter 'r' starts a word, it is rolled as if a double 'rr'.

The letter 'v' is always pronounced as a **soft** English letter 'b'. Try to press your lips together only **very** gently when sayng it.

The letter 'b' is always pronounced as an English letter 'b'.

The two letters 'v' and 'b' are pronounced exactly the same. You may become confused with this if you speak or listen to Italian where the letter 'v' is pronounced as a letter 'v'.

I have mentioned just a few of the many Spanish pronunciation rules. I can tell you that there are pages of rules on how to pronounce Spanish, so you will greatly appreciate that, with our system, you won't need to learn any rules to study and speak Spanish because we explain the pronunciation and emphasis of every word as we teach it to you. It makes it all so easy and reliable. You can be sure that, when you speak words that we teach you, you are pronouncing them and emphasising them as nearly correctly as possible without a personal teacher—and without learning any rules. And, when in Spain, take care not to learn from or copy from anyone who is not a professional teacher. There are many extreme dialects in Portugal, as there are in England and other countries. You must avoid picking up bad pronunciation habits.

Let me give you a couple of examples. In French, the correct pronunciation for the word 'yes' is very similar to 'wee'. But in the French Alps where we go skiing, the local people say 'Way". In Spain, it is a popular colloquial thing to miss off the final letter 'd' at the end of a word. A case in point is the capital city, Madrid. Many people say, 'Madri'. And I hear that habit a lot on television. I have to confess that when I am in Madrid, I sometimes miss off the final 'd' just to 'fit in' with the locals. But it is not correct Spanish pronunciation.

If you ever intend to study a language fully, say taking two years to do so, then you need to start with the pronunciation and emphasis rules right from the word 'go'. Furthermore, you must learn from a professional teacher and practice pronunciation until you are <u>perfect</u> with every rule. Only then should you start to learn.the grammar. Otherwise you will learn many words incorrectly in the first instance and will perpetuate those errors into your speaking as you become more advanced.

2   Speak the 35 verbs.

TO INFINITIVES AND BEYOND

In this chapter, I give you the summary table of the 35 verb-words and, particularly, the infinitive-words that you will eventually need to learn.

Note that I said, 'eventually', because to get started you don't need to learn all of the 105 verb-phrases in the table. I have selected just 35 of them to get you started talking in Spanish on the first day of your holiday—in fact, as you arrive at the airport.

On your arrival, start to get the feel for speaking the language by saying 'please', 'thank you', and 'excuse me' in Spanish at every opportunity. In the words below, emphasise any vowel <u>underlined.</u>

Also, remember when practising phonetic words, to practice them faster and faster until they run into a single word. To take a word at random, the phonetic en-tee-<u>en</u>-doh will give you the required pronunciation but you will not, eventually, say it as if it were four vowels with breaks between. So, it must be practised very slowly together with the emphasis placed on the second <u>en</u>. When you can say it confidently slowly with the correct emphasis, then let it become faster as entee-<u>en</u>doh and become even faster as entee<u>en</u>doh, which you can see is really entiendo.

Here are a few useful words in advance of your main study.

Good morning *is buenos días:* **boo-ay-noss   dee-ass**

Good afternoon is *buenas tardes*: **boo-ay-noss   tar-thes**

[the letter 'r' in tar is sounded.. 'thes' is pronounced as in them]

Good evening is *buenas noches*: **boo-ay-nass   notch-ess**

Good night is *buenas noches*: **boo-ay-nass   notch-ess**

Please is *por favor*: **por   fab-or** *[each or pronounced as in York]*

Thank you is *gracias*: **gra-thee-ass** *[thee as in thief not as in the]*

Excuse me is *discúlpame*: **dee-skool-pah-may** *[pah as in pat]*

Sir is *señor*: **sen-yor** *[yor as in York]*

Madam is *señora*: **sen-yor-ah** *[ah as in pat]*

dee-skool-pah-may   sen-yor *[when getting in someone's way]*

dee-skool-pah-may   sen-yor-ah *[pushing through a crowd]*

THE 35 VERBS

Now, I would like to introduce you to the thirty-five verbs I have selected as being the ones you ultimately need to learn after you have learned the 35 verb-words I have selected for you to start on.

There are, in total, 105 verb-phrases in the table. In itself, that is not an insurmountable challenge to learn, but it is not practical to try and learn all of these words off-by-heart in an academic way without being in Spain and without, therefore, having the immediate need for the words or the ability to practice them when required.

Thus, you will notice, in the table immediately below, I have marked, in **bold print**, the 35 verb-phrases that you will need to use in the early stages of speaking the language more fluently.

At first, **you must learn the 35 bold phonetic verb-phrases in the Verb Table** and then study their usage in the later chapters, during the week or so before you arrive in Italy for your holiday.

Do not bother to learn the Spanish spellings. You are only going to speak, not read or write, so only learn the phonetic pronunciations in your head so that you can speak them.

There is one unusual thing for you to note concerning the Spanish verb 'to be'. In English we just say, "I am", but the Spanish have two forms of the verb 'to be'. One is used for temporary things such as having a cold, feeling ill, being hot, This is 'estar' and you will see it as the first verb of the Prime Verb Table below.

The second one (ser) is used for describing something that is permanent or almost permanent. Such as "I am English". Or, "I am a lawyer", or "my house is big" You won't need 'ser' much, if at all as a beginner. But, nonetheless, you might wish to use it as you progress, so here is a 'special edition' of the 'permanent' verb 'to be', which is outside the Prime Verb Table. Verb 0.

Verb 0
to be   I have *been* (I *was*)   I am
sair   **ay see-doh**   **yo soh-ee**
ser   he *sido*   yo soy

Examples of the use of 'ser' as a verb 'to be' include:

	male	female
I am a lawyer	Soy abogad**o**	abogad**a**.
I am English	Soy inglés (m)	ingles**a** (f)
I am tall	Soy alt**o** (m)	alt**a** (f)

You see that once you are English you are always English and once you have grown tall you are always tall. One is expected to be a lawer for life in the normal run of things, so 'ser' is used for that as well. And so on—anything deemed to be 'permanent'.

There is more than one language having two verbs meaning 'to be'. You may be amused to know that, in Spanish, you can use 'ser' for your general, long-term, weight, but if you have eaten too much over the Christmas holidays and intend to diet it off, then you can use 'estar' to say to a friend that you are fat. Estoy gordo (m).

In the first phase of learning this book, you just need to learn the 35 words shown in bold in the table. The past participles are in italics. The word 'he' is pronounced *'ay'* as in English 'ate'. The word 'yo' means 'I'. It is pronounced as in the English 'toe'.

THE PRIME VERB TABLE

INFINITIVE	PAST	PRESENT
Verb 1		
to be	I have *been* (I *was*)	I am
es-tar	ay *es-taah-doh* [ay as in say]	**yo ess-toy**
estar	he *estado*	yo estoy
Verb 2		
to have	I have *had*	I have
ten-air	ay *ten-ee-doh* [ay as in say]	**yo ten-goh**
tener	he *tenido*	yo tengo
Verb 3		
to want	I have *wanted*	I want
ker-air	ay *ker-ee-doh* [ay as in say]	**yo kee-air-oh**
querer	he *querido*	yo quiero
Verb 4		
to pay	I have *paid*	I pay
pag-ar	**ay *pag-ah-doh***	yo pah-goh
pagar	he *pagado*	yo pago
Verb 5		
to drink	I *drank*	I drink
bay-bear	ay *bay-bee-doh*	yo bay-boh
beber	he *bebido*	yo bebo

INFINITIVE	PAST	PRESENT
Verb 6		
to eat	I have *eaten* (I ate)	I eat
com-air	ay *com-ee-doh*	yo co-mo
comer	he *comido*	yo como
Verb 7		
to do	I have *done* (I did)	I do
ath-air	ay *et-choh*	yo ah-goh
[soft 'th' as in English therapy]		
hacer	he *hecho*	yo hago
Verb 8		
to buy	I have *bought*	I buy
com-prar	ay *com-pradoh*	yo com-proh
comprar	he *comprado*	yo compro
Verb 9		
to reserve	I have *reserved*	I reserve
ray-zair-bar	ay *ray-zair-bah-doh*	yo ray-zair-boh
reservar	he *reservado*	yo reservo
Verb 10		
to look for	I have *looked* for	I look for
boos-car	ay *boos-cah-doh*	**yo boos-coh** *[soft s]*
buscar	he *buscado*	yo busco *[s as sun]*
Verb 11		
to hear	I have *heard*	I hear
au-eer	ay *au-ee-doh*	yo au-ee-goh
oír	he *oído*	yo oigo

INFINITIVE	PAST	PRESENT

Verb 12
to drive — I have *driven* (I drove) — I drive
con-dooth-<u>eer</u> — ay *con-dooth-<u>ee</u>-doh* [*soft 'th'*] — yo con-<u>dooth</u>-coh
conducir — he *conducido* — yo conduzco

Verb 13
to know — I have *known* (I knew) — I know
sah-<u>bear</u> — ay *sah-<u>bee</u>-doh* — **yo say**
saber — he *sabido* — yo sé

Verb 14
to know of — I have *known* of/about it — I know about it
con-oth-<u>air</u> — ay *con-oth-<u>ee</u>-doh* — yo con-<u>oth</u>-koh
[*soft 'th' as in thin*]
conocer — he *conocido* — yo conozco

Verb 15
to give — I have *given* (I gave) — I give
<u>daar</u> — ay *<u>daa</u>-doh* — yo <u>dee</u>
dar — he *dado* — yo di

Verb 16
to hire — I have *hired* — I hire
al-kee-<u>lair</u> — ay *al-kee-<u>lah</u>-doh* — yo al-<u>kee</u>-loh
alquiler — he *alquilado* — yo alquilo

Verb 17
to come — I have *come* (I came) — I come
ben-<u>eer</u> — ay *ben-<u>ee</u>-doh* — **yo ben-goh**
venir — he *venido* — yo vengo

INFINITIVE	PAST	PRESENT

Verb 18
to arrive
yay-gar
llegar

I have *arrived*
ay *yay-gah-doh*
he *llegado*

I arrive
yo yay-goh
yo llego

Verb 19
to go
eer
ir

I have *been* (I went)
ay *ee-doh*
he *ido*

I go
yo boy
yo voy

Verb 20
to return
bol-bear
volver

I have *returned*
ay *boo-el-toh*
he *vuelto*

I return
yo boo-el-boh
yo vuelvo

Verb 21
to open
ab-**reer**
abrir

I have *opened*
ay ab-ee-**air**-toh
he *abierto*

I open
yo **ab**-roh
yo abro

Verb 22
to look (at)
mee-**rar**
mirar

I have *looked* (at)
ay *mee-rah-doh*
he *mirado*

I look (at)
yo **mee**-roh
yo miro

Verb 23
to put
pon-**air**
poner

I have *put*
ay *poo-wes-toh*
he *puesto*

I put
yo **pon**-goh
yo pongo

INFINITIVE	PAST	PRESENT
Verb 24		
to lose	I have *lost*	I lose
pair-<u>dair</u>	**ay *pair-<u>dee</u>-doh***	yo pee-<u>air</u>-doh
perder	he *perdido*	yo pierdo
Verb 25		
to exchange	I have *exchanged*	I exchange
cam-bee-<u>ar</u>	ay *cam-bee-<u>ah</u>-doh*	yo <u>cam</u>-bee-oh
cambiar	he *cambiado*	yo cambio
Verb 26		
to be able	I was *able*	I am able (I can)
pod-<u>air</u>	ay poh-dee-doh	**yo <u>pway</u>-doh**
poder	he *podido*	yo puedo
Verb 27		
to see	I have *seen* (I saw)	I see
<u>bear</u>	ay <u>bee</u>-stoh	**yo <u>bay</u>-oh**
ver	he *visto*	yo veo
Verb 28		
to swim	I have *swum* (I swam)	I swim
nah-<u>dar</u>	ay *nah-<u>dah</u>-doh*	yo <u>nah</u>-doh
nadar	he *nadado*	yo nado
Verb 29		
to sleep	I have *slept*	I sleep
dor-<u>meer</u>	ay dor-<u>mee</u>-doh	yo doo-<u>air</u>-moh
dormir	he *dormido*	yo duermo

INFINITIVE	PAST	PRESENT

Verb 30
to take — I have *taken* (I took) — I take
yay-<u>bar</u> — ay *yay-<u>bah</u>-doh* — yo <u>yay</u>-boh
llevar — he *llevado* — yo llevo

Verb 31
to believe — I have *believed* — I believe
cray-<u>air</u> — ay *cray-<u>ee</u>-doh* — **yo <u>cray</u>-oh**
creer — he *creído* — yo creo

Verb 32
to understand — I have *understood* — I understand
kom-prend-<u>air</u> — ay *kom-pren-<u>dee</u>-doh* — **yo com-<u>pren</u>-doh**
comprender — he *comprendido* — yo comprendo

Verb 33
to walk — I have *walked* — I walk
cam-ee-<u>naar</u> — ay *cam-ee-<u>nah</u>-doh* — yo cah-<u>mee</u>-noh
caminar — he *caminado* — yo camino

Verb 34
to listen — I have *listened* — I listen
es-koo-<u>chaar</u> — ay *es-koo-<u>chah</u>-doh* — yo es-<u>koo</u>-choh
escuchar — he *escuchado* — yo escucho

Verb 35
to finish — I have *finished* — I finish
tair-mee-<u>naar</u> — **ay tair-mee-<u>nah</u>-doh** — yo tair-<u>mee</u>-noh
terminar — he *terminado* — yo termino

The primary verb-phrases you **must** learn are shown in **bold** font in the Prime Verb Table above. You will notice that there are 17 bold infinitives, 5 bold past participles (italicised), and 13 bold present tenses to learn. When you have done that, you will be ready to start talking!

That's a total of 35 new 'verb-phrases to learn as a 'must'. That should take you, say, three days at about twelve phrases a day. It is not a lot. You don't have to learn 105, only 35 in the first instance. Go for it.

When you have learned those 35 phrases, <u>the next 60 pages contain nothing much new</u>. All they contain is help and explanations for how to fit those 35 phrases together so that you can talk your holiday language. When you have learned the 35 verb-phrases, you have done the majority of the work and you can simply enjoy going through the next 60 pages, seeing how easily and interestingly those phrases fit together to let you speak Spanish fluently on holiday.

You need to be able to say all 35 bold-printed word-phrases from memory without this book in your hands.

Do a little mental rôle-playing. Imagine yourself on holiday, going swimming, asking for something, reserving a table for dinner at a restaurant, telling someone that you have lost something. These mind-images will help you to pull the words out of your head. It makes the job much easier if you do this imaginative role playing.

Then spend the rest of the week studying Chapters 3 to 8 and memorising how to fit the words together, one with another.

Don't forget, 'yo' is pronounced as English 'toe', 'he' is pronounced 'ay' as in English 'ate', 'th' is sounded soft as in 'thin', and the letter 's' is pronounced softly as in 'sun'.

In the next three chapters, I take you through the 17 infinitives, then the 5 past participles, and finally the 13 present tense verb-phrases. Following that, in Chapter 6, I show you how to construct a 'future sentence'.

3 Speak the infinitive.

TO ENJOY SPEAKING SPANISH

THE SEVENTEEN INFINITIVE EXAMPLES FROM THE PRIME VERB TABLE

Let's look at the seventeen infinitive examples I selected from the prime table as being the potentially most useful for you when on holiday. They are numbered below according to their prime table listing.

I list them, sequentially, and show you why I chose each one and how to use it.

First, before giving examples, the most common use that you will have for the infinitive is to say when you want something. It is no surprise to see that the verb 'to want' is number 3 on the Prime Verb Table list. It is there because of the present tense use of the phrase, "I want". This is the most-used phrase that you will need on holiday. After all, you are always saying I want a cup of tea, or a beer, or a cake. Those are objects, but you can also want things done—meaning actions, which is where our verbs come in.

Asking for an action is achieved by using the present tense of Verb 3 (volere), using **yo kee-air-oh** (I want), to say that you want some action, followed by an infinitive. (The action you want done.)

Yo kee-<u>air</u>-oh **com-<u>air</u>**	Verb 6	I want to eat
Yo kee-<u>air</u>-oh **com-<u>prar</u>**	Verb 8	I want to buy
Yo kee-<u>air</u>-oh **na-<u>dar</u>**	Verb 28	I want to swim

And that's it. That's all you have to do. **Just put 'Yo kee-<u>air</u>-oh' in front of any infinitive and you can ask for any action you like.** In the case of the Roberts system, you have a choice of 35 action verb infinitives. But, in reality, as you progress, you can add the infinitive of any verb you may need at any given time in the future.

Of course, as you will see when we look at each of the 17 important infinitives I chose, you can make the Yo kee-<u>air</u>-oh expression much more informative and precise just by adding a final word or two after the action verb.

Just as brief examples of refinement, you might wish to say:

Yo Quiero **comer** esta noch-ay	I want to eat this evening.
Yo quiero **comprar** es-oh	I want to buy that (point to it)
Yo quiero **nadar** ah-ora	I want to swim now.

Try not saying the 'yo' as you become confident. Now that you have got the idea, let's look through the 17 infinitives one at a time and explore how you can use each one on holiday in Spain.

1	**to be**	Pronounced: **es-<u>tar</u>**
		Written: estar

You can use this infinitive with 'quiero' whenever you want to be somewhere. **Try not saying the 'yo' as you progress.**

For example, say you are by the pool and you are starting to burn a bit; so you wish to have your sun lounger moved to a shady spot, you can look up the word for 'the shade' (la <u>som</u>-brah) and say to the pool attendant:

'Quiero' is pronounced: **Kee-<u>air</u>-oh**
Quiero	estar	a	la sombra,	por fabor
I want	to be	in	the shade	please

- - - - - - - - - - oOo - - - - - - - - - -

2   **to have**   Pronounced: **ten-<u>air</u>**
                                     Written: tener

You can use this infinitive with 'Quiero' whenever you want to have something.

For example, say you are in the café and the waiter comes up to you, then you can ask for anything off the menu. There are two ways. If you know the name of the thing you want, you can say it, or alternatively, if you don't know its name in Spanish, you can simply point to it on the menu and use the word 'eso', meaning 'that'. Eso is pronounced **<u>es</u>-oh**, where s is a 'soft s' as in 'Esso'.

Quiero	**ten-<u>air</u>**	pas-<u>tel</u>	por fab-<u>or</u>
I want	to have	cake	please

or, put more simply, Quiero pas<u>tel</u> por fab<u>or</u>
or
Quiero	**<u>es</u>-oh**	por fab-<u>or</u>	
I want	that	please	(point to the menu or object)

or
Quiero **ten-<u>air</u>** oon p<u>o</u>co m<u>á</u>s por fab-<u>or</u>
I want to have a little more please
(when the waitress only gives you one scoop of chips and you want more) Actually, for me, speaking reasonable Spanish, if I see that I want more on my plate, I just look at the waiter and say:

Un poco más, por favor   (**Oon p<u>oh</u>-koh mass por fa-<u>bor</u>**)
And no more is needed.

When you are in a café or in a bar, and you want to get the bill, you wouldn't bother with **ten-<u>air</u>**. You would catch the waiter's eye and say:

La cuenta por favor   (**La <u>kwen</u>-tah por fa-<u>bor</u>**)
The bill please

or, since in most Spanish cafés, the waiter will have left the bill on a saucer when he delivered your drinks and food, you need to see verb 4, **pag-<u>ar</u>**, (to pay), below.

- - - - - - - - - - oOo - - - - - - - - - -

4   **to pay**   Pronounced: **pag-<u>ar</u>**
Written: pagar

Of course, the moment always comes in a café or bar when you need to pay the bill. If the waiter has already left your bill in a saucer when he served you, then you would be a little silly to ask for the bill. So, you would need to catch his eye and say:

Yo kee-<u>air</u>-oh   **pag-<u>ar</u>**   *por fabor*
I   want   to pay   pl*ea*se

(You can beneficially wave your credit card to attract his attention if you don't want to say anything. He will get the message and bring a card machine to your table. (But use cash for the 10% tip.)

For ordering in Spanish cafés and bars, see our accompanying book, "Learn 35 Words to Speak Spanish".

- - - - - - - - - - oOo - - - - - - - - - -

5   **to drink**   Pronounced: **bay-<u>bear</u>**
                      Written: beber

If you order for yourself, you can look at the waiter and say:

For   to drink   I   want   a   beer   / that!
Para **bay-<u>bear</u>** yo kee-<u>air</u>-oh oona ther-<u>bay</u>-thah / <u>e</u>-soh!
['e-soh' means 'that', so when you say 'e-soh', point to the item you want, on the drinks list] [the 'th's are soft as in 'thanks']

- - - - - - - - - - oOo - - - - - - - - - -

6   **to eat**   Pronounced: **com-<u>air</u>**
                     Written: comer

If you order for yourself, you can look at the waiter and say:

For   to eat   I want   soup /   chicken /   that! *[point]*
para **com-<u>air</u>,**   quiero   soh-pah / poh-yoh /   <u>eso</u>! *[point]*

- - - - - - - - - - oOo - - - - - - - - - -

7   **to do**   Pronounced: **ah-ther** *[ther as in therapy]*
                              Written: hacer

Whatever you want to do, you can employ this infinitive *hacer*:

```
Yo quiero      hacer      eso
Yo kee-air-oh  ah-ther    es-oh!    [th is soft as in 'thanks']
I    want      to do      that!     [point to something]
```

And if you want to do it again, you can add the words, 'de nuevo'. De nuevo means 'again', and is pronounced **deh noo-ay-boh**
Yo kee-air-oh ah-ther eso **deh noo-ay-boh**!

- - - - - - - - - - oOo - - - - - - - - - -

8   **to buy**   Pronounced: **com-prar** *[ar as in car]*
                                Written: comprar *[pronounce the final r]*

And now we come to the most favourite and popular of all our holiday activities—shopping! Yes, we all want to buy something. If you are in a shop, you may not know the names for any of the things they are selling, so the very best thing to do is to point to something and say:

```
Yo kee-air-oh  com-prar   es-oh!
I    want      to buy     that!
```

Or, if you are not too sure that you will buy the object, you can ask to look at it first (See verb 22).

```
Yo kee-air-oh  mee-rar    es-oh    por fa-bor.
I    want      to look at that     please.
```

You will have no trouble buying something on holiday if you know the simple 'sa' rule. Learn it and use it every day!

Or, in the event that you are looking for something but it is not visible in the shop, then you need to look up the name for the thing you want in your dictionary before you go shopping. Learn the name first. Let's say it is a belt that you are looking for (you have eaten so much on holiday that your old belt has become too tight). The word for belt in Spanish is cinturón, pronounced **theen-toor-on**. You can go into a shop and say:

Yo kee-<u>air</u>-oh	comp-<u>rar</u>	**oon**	**theen-toor-on**
I	want to buy	a	belt.

Of course, it would be sensible to look up the word for brown (ma-<u>rron</u>) or black (<u>neh</u>-groh) before going shopping. Notice that I write ma-rron with a double rr because you shoud roll the rr.

Yo kee-<u>air</u>-oh	comp-<u>rar</u>	oon	theen-toor-<u>on</u>	**ma-<u>rron</u>**
I	want to buy	a	belt	brown

There is a further tip here in relation to feminine and masculine words in Spanish. If I don't tell you differently, you can optionally use the masculine word **oon** before objects. That is better than having to learn what to put in front of every different object's name. You will still be understood, don't worry. In a shop, they won't mind your grammar slipping a bit because you are, at least, trying to speak Spanish and you will be a valued customer.

- - - - - - - - - - oOo - - - - - - - - - -

9	**to reserve**	Pronounced: **ray-zair-<u>bar</u>** *['zair' as hair]*
		Written: reservar

You will want to reserve a table frequently on holiday. I do, often. Of course, if you are in your hotel or a holiday resort in general, you will be able to reserve your table in English without any trouble. However, sometimes, when we are touring in the countryside, in a small village and we want to be sure that we will have a table booked for lunch, I will drop into a restaurant and reserve a table. If you wish to do this, then it's best to look up the Spanish words for 12.45, 1.00, and 1.15, pm (See Chapter 8). Then you can reserve the table for a particular time. And, you will need the words for 'for one—para <u>oon</u>-oh' or 'for two people—para <u>doss</u>'. Not too difficult at all if you wish to learn a little more Spanish and speak it. That would be most rewarding.

Yo kee-<u>air</u>-oh	**ray-zair-<u>bar</u>**	<u>oon</u>-ah	<u>may</u>-sah	para <u>doss</u>.
I	want	to reserve	a	table	for	two.

- - - - - - - - - - oOo - - - - - - - - - -

16   **to hire**   Pronounced: **al-kee-<u>laar</u>**   *['aar' as in car]*
                         Written: alquilar

It is unlikely that you will need to speak Spanish to hire a car at the airport or in town, because it is almost certain that the hire company will speak the relevant English. However, for less important things, when you are in the countryside, you might wish to hire a bicycle or snow shoes, or some other small item that does not involve the technical complications of insurance, deposits, and the like. In that event, you can easily say:

Yo kee-<u>air</u>-oh	**al-kee-<u>laar</u>**	<u>oo</u>-nah	bee-thee-<u>kleh</u>-tah.
I	want	to hire	a	bicycle. *[th as in thin]*

You can ask to hire anything as long as you have looked up the name in advance. Or you can simply resort to pointing and saying:

Yo	kee-<u>air</u>-oh	**al-kee-<u>laar</u>**	<u>oo</u>-noh	**a-<u>see</u>** !	por fa-<u>bor</u>
I	want	to hire	one	like that!	please.

That's a handy phrase, isn't it? "One like that"—"uno asi" can be used anywhere and for anything. I suggest you learn it.

- - - - - - - - - - oOo - - - - - - - - - -

17   **to come**   Pronounced: **ben-<u>eer</u>**
                      Written: venir

Perhaps you have taken an item to a shop to be repaired, or some clothes to a dry-cleaner's shop. Then you might wish to confirm to the shop attendant that you will come back to collect your item at a particular time or date. You will need to look up the word you need in advance, but here are a couple of options.

Yo	<u>day</u>-boh	**ben-<u>eer</u>**	<u>es</u>-ta	<u>notch</u>-ay?
I	must	to come	this	evening?

oh	man-<u>yah</u>-nah	oh	mar-tez?
or	tomorrow?	or	Tuesday?

Chapter 8 of this book (Useful Stuff) contains a list of dates and days of the week and other optional words for this purpose.

- - - - - - - - - - oOo - - - - - - - - - -

18   **to arrive**   Pronounced: **yay-<u>gar</u>**   *['yay' as in day]*
                       Written: llegar

This is most useful when asking if you can be at a certain place at a certain time. Say, for example, you want to check that you can check into your hotel at a certain time, you can use this infinitive. Or, if you have booked a city bus tour and you wish to check what time you must turn up at the bus stop. You can ask the question:

Yo	<u>day</u>-boh	**yay-<u>gar</u>**	ah-<u>kee</u>	a	las dos	deh	la	<u>tar</u>-day?
I	must	to arrive	here	at	two	in	the	afternoon?

la <u>oo</u>-na   is   1 o'clock
las tress   is   3 o'clock

(Chapter 8 contains information on how to speak clock times.)

- - - - - - - - - - oOo - - - - - - - - - -

19   **to go**   Pronounced: **<u>eer</u>**
                         Written: ir

Perhaps you wish to tell someone that you must leave a place.

Yo	<u>day</u>-boh	**<u>eer</u>**	a-<u>ora</u>
I	must	to go	now.

Or, if you have been kept waiting somewhere for a long time, you might say:

Yo	kee-<u>air</u>-oh	**<u>eer</u>**	<u>pron</u>-toe.
I	want	to go	soon.

- - - - - - - - - - oOo - - - - - - - - - -

20   **to return**   Pronounced: **bol-bear**
              Written: volver

If you have booked a taxi, or some other transport, you might wish to tell the driver when you want to return. So, you can say:

Yo	kee-<u>air</u>-oh	**bol-<u>bear</u>**	ah-<u>kee</u>	a	las <u>theen</u>-koh	por fa-<u>bor</u>.
I	want	to return	here	at	five o'clock	please.

or, you might turn it into a question by using your tone of voice. If you raise the pitch of your voice on the last two or three words, you can turn just about any positive statement into a question. For example, perhaps you have asked the hotel to arrange a taxi to take you somewhere and bring you back later. Say that, when you are being dropped off, you wish to confirm with the driver that he is going to pick you up at five o'clock, you can say the following as a question by raising your voice and even asking 'yes?'.

Yo	<u>day</u>-boh	**bol-<u>bear</u>**	ah-<u>kee</u>	a	las <u>theen</u>-coh?	See?
I	must	to return	here	at	five o'clock?	Yes?

(Clock times and numbers are listed with their pronunciations in Chapter 8 of this book.)

- - - - - - - - - - oOo - - - - - - - - - -

25   **to exchange**   Pronounced: **cam-bee-<u>ar</u>** *[ar as in car]*
                 Written: cambiar

This could be a useful verb infinitive for you. I envisage the possibility that you have purchased some small item in the local market and have found it to be faulty or not correct in some way.

Yo kee-<u>air</u>-oh **cam-bee-ar** <u>es</u>to por <u>oh</u>-troh por fa-<u>vor</u>.
I   want   to exchange   this   for   another   please.

It seems to me that you could use this construction for a variety of situations. For example, if you find that something is damaged in your hotel room, or you find you have a dirty fork at your dinner table, you could ask for it to be exchanged for another one. Or, at the airport, in a bank or a shop when you see the sign that says, 'cambio' and ask to exchange Sterling for Euros. Simply hold up your money and say, "Yo kee-<u>air</u>-oh **cam-bee-ar** <u>es</u>to". It is a potentially very useful construction for an otherwise difficult-to-describe situation.

- - - - - - - - - - oOo - - - - - - - - - -

28   **to swim**   Pronounced: **<u>naa</u>-jay**   *['naa' as in bar]*
                     Written: nager   *[say j soft as in pleasure]*

This is not a verb infinitive for an emergency, but you might use it in a variety of conversational situations with a Spanish-speaking person on holiday, if you get far enough to start dipping your metaphorical toes into conversation. Or you can use it to chat to your holiday partner. For example::

Yo   kee-<u>air</u>-oh   **nah-<u>dar</u>**   <u>es</u>-ta   <u>tar</u>-day
I   want   to swim   this   afternoon.

<u>Always</u> emphasise the <u>last</u> vowel of an infinitive, and start to leave out the 'yo' as you become more fluent and confident.

- - - - - - - - - - oOo - - - - - - - - - -

29   **to sleep**   Pronounced: **<u>dor</u>-meer**   *['dor' as in for]*
                        Written: dormir   *[but sound the 'r'!]*

Again, a verb that is unlikely to be used in an emergency, but you might say it to a room-maid who calls at your room to tidy it before you have risen in the morning. Perhaps you have jet-lag or perhaps you have partied too late the night before?

Dee-<u>skool</u>-pay,   yo kee-<u>air</u>-oh   dor-<u>meer</u>   a-<u>or</u>-a
Pardon/excuse me   I   want   to sleep   now.

- - - - - - - - - - oOo - - - - - - - - - -

33   **to walk**   Pronounced: **cam-ee-<u>nar</u>**
                        Written: caminar

Again, more for early conversational purposes, you could try speaking to the hotel receptionist or a member of staff, even though they will speak good English.

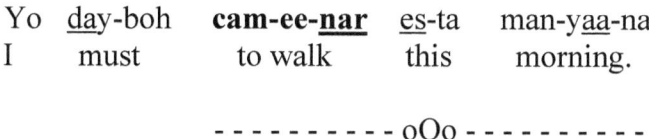

Yo   <u>day</u>-boh   **cam-ee-<u>nar</u>**   <u>es</u>-ta   man-<u>yaa</u>-na
I   must   to walk   this   morning.

- - - - - - - - - - oOo - - - - - - - - - -

And there is one final, and very useful, thing that I would like to tell you that you can use the infinitive for—now that you have learned quite a few. That is the ability to use it for asking general questions as to whether something is so or not.

That may sound confusing, but, it is actually easy to do and easy to understand when I give you some examples. You only have to know that the Spanish word para means 'to' or 'for'.

Now, let's look at how you can ask useful questions with just these two: infinitive + useful word   and   para + infinitive.

Say you are in a market and you see something on a stall but you are not sure if that thing is for sale, you can simply ask the stall-owner, "para bend-<u>air</u>? (for to sell?)." The verb 'vender' (bend-air) is the infinitive meaning 'to sell'. If you place 'para' in front of it, you make a generic question: "to sell?". (Literally you ask "for to sell"?) Just look how you can simplify many things:

Do I pay here?	Pagar aquí?	**pah-<u>gar</u> ah-<u>kee</u>**
Do I pay later?	Pagar despu<u>és</u>?	dess-poo-<u>ess</u>
Do I pay in advance?	Pagar por adelan<u>ta</u>do?	adel-an-<u>ta</u>-doh

For rent/hire?	Para alquilar?	**al-kee-<u>lar</u>**
For exchange?	Para cambiar?	**cam-bee-<u>ar</u>**
For taking away?	Para llevar?	**yay-<u>bar</u>**

It's amazingly flexible. You can ask many complex questions with just these two formats. You can find any infinitive in a dictionary. Go to the verb you want in your dictionary—perhaps you want to ask if you can enter to an exhibition through a door that is only marked in Spanish. You look up the word "Enter" in your small dictionary. It will give you the infinitive, "Ent<u>r</u>ar". So you can point to the door and ask, "Ent<u>r</u>ar aquí?", pronounced **"En-<u>traar</u> a-<u>kee</u>"** where 'aqui' means 'here'.

It is best to precede such questions with 'excuse me'. Discúlpame. **Dee-<u>skool</u>-pah-may** so that the person can hear that you are a foreigner about to speak Spanish and they can listen closely.

4 Speak the past tense.

I HAVE ENJOYED SPEAKING SPANISH

WHAT IS A TENSE?

Next, we have the word, "Tense". A verb tells you about something that takes place or occurs. The 'tense' tells you WHEN that thing takes place or occurs. In very general terms, things have either taken place in the past, are taking place now in the present, or will take place in the future. So, verb tenses for beginners divide into past, present, and future.

THE PAST TENSE

The complication comes when we have to make fine distinctions between different types of past, different types of present, and different types of future. How can there be different types of these verbs? you might well ask. Let's have a look in English before swimming into a sea of Spanish verbs.

In English, we have past verb constructions such as, "I ate", "I was eating", "I did eat", "I used to eat", and so on. You can easily imagine how you would use those quite commonly in English. In the process of my reducing all those to one simple past tense, I have to recognise that it will be a compromise. It will not be at all sophisticated and will not express a fine nuance as to the detail of the past activity. I gave this considerable thought and ended up avoiding the obvious. That obvious solution is to simply say, "I went". It sounds inviting but, I realised that it actually entailed more learning work than the option I chose for you.

For my simple 'past', I chose "I have been", or "I have eaten", or "I have bought". That, ultimately, will save you a significant block of learning.

So, I decided to uses a word called a **"Past Participle"**. Another enigmatic phrase. I can shorten it to **PP** to save space. First, I have to explain it so that you can understand what it is.

Let's look at it in English. If I say to you, "I have been…" you can see that this phrase has two parts: 'I have' and 'been'. Both are verbs. Have is the present part of 'to have' and 'been' is the past participle of 'to be'. So, 'have been' is called a compound verb because it is formed from two bits of two verbs.

Both of these turn out to be important for the Roberts verb system. The PP we are talking about at the moment is 'been', which is the past participle of the verb 'to be'.

Let's look at a number of examples, all incorporating the verb 'to have' with the past participle of different verbs. Here we go:

I have *been*.   (*been* is the PP of 'to be'.)
I have *eaten*.   (*eaten* is the PP of 'to eat'.)
I have *walked*.   (*walked* is the PP of 'to walk'.)

You get the picture now. You are familiar, I am sure, with dozens more.

This is the construction that I chose to adopt for the Roberts system. So, it forms our simple 'past tense' for *all the 35 verbs* you are going to study and learn. Let's look at it with fancy words:

1st person singular + 'have' + past participle.
e.g.   I   have   eaten

If you had seen that without the explanations it would have looked complicating and forbidding. But, now you know exactly what it means. It means:

I have lived in London, for example.

Which I tell you that you can now use to substitute for

I lived in London.
I used to live in London.
I have lived in London.
I lived briefly in London.
And so on.

We can also say:
I have been.
I have laughed.
I have run.
I have flown.
I have danced.

This makes the past tense incredibly easy for us. One easy construction.

You only have to learn the Spanish words for 'I have' and then learn one PP word for every verb in the 35 verbs and you have cracked it! You now know how to use the past tense for every one of the 35 verbs and for any other verb that you choose to learn subsequently.

Examples:

I have *looked*.   *looked* is the PP of the verb "to look".
I have *drunk*.   *drunk* is the PP of the verb "to drink".
I have *lost*.   *lost* is the PP of the verb 'to lose'.

And that is all there is to it.

You have already learned 'I have' in Spanish, from the Prime Verb Table; it is Verb 2.

Let's look at it in Spanish. What is 'I have' in Spanish"? It is "he", **pronounced, 'ay'**—but only when you use 'I have' as indicating the past. *[I need to tell you, in passing, that when "I have" is used in the possessive sense, meaning, I own something, then the word is "tengo".]* I have a cold, I have a pain, I have an apple, I have any object. All use 'tengo' from Verb 2, 'ten<u>er</u>'.

You learn 35 past participles in Spanish and you can now say the past tense of all of those verbs. Just learning 1 + 35 words at most—probably less. Not too difficult at all.

And what is the PP of com<u>er</u>, 'to eat'? It is, "co<u>mi</u>do"—eaten.

So, we know how to say the past phrase, I have eaten >>> He comido, which is pronounced, **"ay com-<u>ee</u>-doh".**

And the same simple procedure follows in each of our 35 verbs.

I have slept   **"ay dor-<u>mee</u>-doh"**   written: He dormido. *dormido* is the PP of infinitive dormir, 'to sleep'. *[sound the r in dor]*

I have eaten **"ay com-ee-doh"** written: He comido.
Comido is the PP of infinitive comer, 'to eat'.

I have been **"ay es-tah-doh"** written: He estado
estado is PP of infinitive estar 'to be'.

I have wanted **" ay ker-ee-doh"** written: He querido.
querido is the PP of infinitive querer, 'to want'.

I gave you the full list in the Prime Verb Table in Chapter 2.

Ultimately, you may well learn the whole list, but in the meantime, on the basis of your likely immediate usage, despite the fact that it is so easy to learn, I have selected just 5 out of 35 possible Past Participles for you to start with. The reason being that, on holiday, you will not tend to need the past tense until you have learned enough fluency and vocabulary to start entering into conversation with people. But we must start somewhere.

Let's look at 5 Past Participle examples and how to use them. We have already learned how to say the non-possessive 'he', "I have". In Spanish it is pronounced 'ay' as in the English word 'ate'.

Five 'Must learn' Past Participles. (PPs)

4   **he** *pagado*   Pronounced: **ay** *pag-ah-doh* *['ay' as ate]*
     PP is ***pagado***   Meaning: I have paid

It can happen in a number of different scenarios that, on holiday in a foreign country, you will need to assure a waiter, a ticket collector, an art gallery guard, a cinema attendant, or a beach supervisor, that you have paid for your ticket. So, the first thing that you need to know is that the Spanish words for 'a ticket' are 'oon boleto', pronounced, **bol-ay-toh**. *[emphasise the **ay**.]*

So, the expected dialogue is not too difficult. Perhaps an official will simply come up to you and say, "Boleto?" You can say, "See" (Yes), and show him/her your ticket. Nothing else to say. Or, you could say, "See, tengo uhn boleto". Which, by now, you know means "Yes, I have a ticket". That is fine as well. Or, perhaps, under slightly different circumstances, you may feel it more appropriate to say, "See, ay pagaado". Which says, "Yes, I have paid". At that point, if your paying is being queried, you are best advised to remain very polite and to produce your ticket or your shop receipt. And then there will be no problem and your holiday will continue just fine. It's a good idea to learn **ay pa-gaa-doh** really well. *(Sometimes, for tourists, they just say the word 'ticket?'.)* *[Remember that '**ay**' is pronounced as in 'ate']*

- - - - - - - - - - oOo - - - - - - - - - -

9   **ay reservado**   Pronounced: **ay *ray-zair-bah-doh***
        PP is ***reservado***   Meaning: I have reserved

And, here is another example that you will need to know and use all the time on holiday. We have already covered, in the section on the infinitives, how to reserve a table in a restaurant. However, when you turn up at the restaurant, the waiter, receptionist or Maître D, will always ask if you have a reservation. If it is in your hotel or a town restaurant, the odds are heavily that they will speak to you in English. I suggest that you respond in English accordingly and, considering that you are likely to be drinking alcohol, it is better not to become embroiled in an attempted conversation at this stage of your language learning capabilities.

If you are in a small village in the countryside where it becomes clear that the owner and staff really don't speak any English, then that is where you will shine. Note that they will smile and probably ask:

Tiene una reserva?
Tee-en-ay oona ray-zer-bah?
You have a reservation?
or
Hay alguna reserva?
I al-goo-nah ray-zer-bah? *[Pronouncing I as in eye]*
There is some reservation?
Concentrate on listening for the word ray-zer-bah? '

I mention these suggestions so that you may expect and anticipate some request of that kind and be able to catch it when the waiter/owner speaks Spanish at six-hundred km/ hour! Eventually, after all that, you can say, **"See, ay ray-zair-bah-doh"**, which—as you now know—means, "Yes, I have reserved." Then say your name; they will surely need that.
Anticipation in context is the key to any linguistic interaction.

And, you would be advised to then restrict yourself to pointing at the menu when the waiter comes to take your order. You can say, **"yo kee-air-oh esso "** as you point. Which means, "I want that".

Our sister book, "Learn 35 **Words** to Speak Spanish" covers the café and restaurant scene much more thoroughly than my suggestions here.

- - - - - - - - - - oOo - - - - - - - - - -

19 he *ido* Pronounced: "**ay** *ee-doh*" *[ay as in 'ate']*
PP is *ido* Meaning: I have gone

[You will recall that the Spanish word 'he' (pronounced 'ay' as in the English word 'ate') does not mean literally 'I have' an object, as in the case of tengo (Verb 2). It simply indicates the past in the same way that we say, in English, 'I have' been.]

"**ay** *ee-doh*" can mean 'I have gone' or 'I went'. Of course, as we have discussed before, there are many more sophisticated ways of using specialised past tenses in Spanish, but the Robertson system is to learn the minimum possible while communicating reliably. If you say **ay** *ee-doh*, any Spanish speaking person knows perfectly that you are referring to you having gone, using the past tense.

Let's look at some examples of usage.

You might simply be partaking in a tentative conversation during which you wish to tell someone that you have been somewhere. You might wish to say, "Yes, I have been to Madrid".

Sí,	**he**	*ido*	en	Madrid.
Yes,	I have	been	to	Madrid.

(Spanish people are often interested to know this because it opens up other avenues of chat. Especially, you can expect the next question to ask how you liked Madrid—or similar.)

It is up to you and your progress in learning Spanish as to how much you choose to, or try to, embellish upon your answer.

- - - - - - - - - - oOo - - - - - - - - - -

24   **he perdido**   Pronounced: **ay** *pair-dee-doh*
     PP is *perdido*   Meaning: I have lost

I have included this example because losing something on holiday is a common occurrence and it may involve talking to people in a local market, or a village, or to the room-cleaning staff in your hotel, few of whom will speak English. If you have lost something in your bedroom, you may choose to wait and speak to the cleaning lady but if the item is valuable, you are best to go and immediately report the missing item to the floor manager at your hotel—speaking in English. There is nothing to stop you telling the room cleaner, in Spanish, that you have lost something if it is just a small item of little value. That will give you the opportunity to use this Past Participle verb-word.

He perdido mi cepillo de dientes
Ay   pair-dee-doh mee   theh-pee-yoh deh dee-entes / libro
I have   lost   my   brush   of   teeth   / book.
                                            (toothbrush)

This is an occasion where you will have plenty of time, in advance, to look up the word you need in your small dictionary.

Incidentally, make sure that you buy a small dictionary that is English-to-Spanish and Spanish-to-English—not just one-way.

- - - - - - - - - - oOo - - - - - - - - - -

And, finally, the last of the five.

35   **he terminado** Pronounced: **ay tair-mee-nah-doh**
       PP is ***terminado***   Meaning: I have finished

Oh, yes. I use this continually on holiday abroad whenever I am in a restaurant or a café.

It is a necessity for the waiter/waitress in a restaurant to come to your table and ask whether you have finished your soup, main course, or sweet. They may actually ask, "Terminado?" or they may ask it in English, "Finished?" Clearly, if you are in the countryside and the waiter asks you "Terminado?" you can happily reply, 'Sí, he terminado'—**"See, ay tair-mee-nah-doh!"** followed by 'gracias', pronounced **"gra-thee-as"**. This means, "Yes, I have finished. Thank you". [Note that the 'th' in **thee** is sounded as in the English words 'thief', or thin—not as in 'this' or 'then'.

However, even if you are in an expensive restaurant or your hotel dining room, this is an opportunity when you can reply in Spanish. It is polite to do so, and saying, "Yes I have finished, thank you", does not invite any further conversation. The waiter/waitress will simply sweep the used plates away and bring the next course. Excellent.

Additionally, during any meal or evening drinking session, it is always good to sprinkle your interaction with the waiter with **"por fabor"**—Please, and **"gra-thee-as"**—Thank you. I don't want you to feel that I think you need reminding of your manners. No, it is just that I want you to say foreign words as much as possible, whenever possible, in order to reinforce that this is a real language that you can speak without thinking about it. Use small words like yes, no, please, thank you, all the time in Spanish because they will encourage you to say some more and increase your familiarity with the use of the language.

Some continental people find it amusing that the English say, 'Please', and 'Thank you', so much. However, it is fine to amuse other people by apparently being eccentric, and being too polite can never do any harm. Also, it gives you speaking practice.

[Incidentally, it is just my personal preference, but I always tend to tip drinks and bar staff; it is difficult to imagine how you can go wrong in doing that as long as you do it quietly and without a big fuss.]

It will not be too long before you can learn to say, "Yes, my husband and I have been to Madrid many times. Usually in the Spring because Madrid is so beautiful at that time of year."

It certainly is. Believe it!

Here it is in Spanish: "Sí, mi marido y yo hemos estado en Madrid muchas veces. Normalmente en primavera porque Madrid es muy bonito en esa época del año".

If you chose, it would not be more than a couple of years of study before you could write and speak that kind of Spanish with ease.

There are two main downsides to spending several years learning a language. The first is that people rarely feel that they can commit the time to learning another and another. So, they just learn the one language and find themselves torn between always returning to that one country and going to other countries where they are ignorant of the language. The second is that, having learned a large vocabulary, many verbs, and much detailed grammar, they rarely use it all and they rapidly forget most of it.

I have found that, what people really want on holiday is to be able to speak and not to read or write. The Roberts system, concentrates on speaking the language only. And, by committing only a few weeks of study per language, you can learn three or more 'holiday languages' with ease. You have the added benefit that, because you only learn what you need and use, you forget very little and you can easily re-learn it in just one day prior to your next holiday.

So, go to Spain, nip over the border into France and Portugal using our French, Spanish and Portuguese books. And when you go skiing in the Austrian Alps next winter, take our German book. Speak English and four foreign languages with ease. Of course, only at holiday standard, but that's all you really need, isn't it?

It is so much more fun to speak four new languages rather than just one.

5 Speak the present tense.

I ENJOY SPEAKING SPANISH

THE PRESENT TENSE

You might guess that the present tense would be absolutely simple, but you would be mistaken. In any sophisticated language there are a number of different subtle forms of the present tense. Even in the Roberts cut-down system, there are 35 different present tense verb-words to learn. So, to start with, to help you 'get going', I have selected just 13 of them, which I believe are 'must learn' words.

You might think that the present tense should just describe what we are doing right now. But, it also describes different times over which we are doing something right now. Let's see a few examples.

I go.　　　　　Simple present tense.
I am going.　　Present tense over a longer period.
I am in the process of going　Over an even longer period.
I go! Used in the affirmative to confirm that you are going.

Here are some examples taken from the Primary Verb Table.
I go.　　　　Yo voy　　*['voy' pronounced 'boy']*
I eat　　　　Yo como

I sleep   Yo duermo
I see   Yo veo

So, we can simply use Yo, which means 'I' in English, and we add on any one of 35 present tense verb-words to make a present tense verb phrase.

To start you off, however, I shall only take you through the 13 pre-selected present tense words that you need right now, and tell you why I have chosen them from the Prime Verb Table in Chapter 2. The verb numbers are those verbs selected from the Table and so are, naturally, not fully sequential. First, here is the summary list of present-tense verb statements.

'Must learn' Present Tense Words.

1   **yo estoy**   Pronounced: **yo ess-toy**
                           Meaning: I am

2   **yo tengo**   Pronounced: **yo ten-goh**
                           Meaning: I have

3   **yo quiero**   Pronounced: **yo kee-air-oh**
                           Meaning: I want

10   **yo busco**   Pronounced: **yo boos-coh** *[soft s as in sun]*
                           Meaning: I look for, or I seek

13   **yo sé**   Pronounced: **yo say**
                           Meaning: I know

17   **yo vengo**   Pronounced: **yo ben-goh**
                           Meaning: I come, or I am coming

18	**yo llego**	Pronounced: **yo yay-go** *['ll' always as y]*
		Meaning: I arrive

19	**yo voy**	Pronounced: **yo boy**
		Meaning: I go

20	**yo vuelvo**	Pronounced: **yo boo-el-boh**
		Meaning: I return

26	**yo puedo**	Pronounced: **yo pway-doh**
		Meaning: I am able

27	**yo veo**	Pronounced: **yo bay-oh**
		Meaning: I see

31	**yo pienso**	Pronounced: **yo pee-en-soh**
		Meaning: I think

32	**yo comprendo**	Pronounced: **yo com-pren-doh**
		Meaning: I understand

How to make a statement negative.

Yo quiero   I want (a thing)   e.g. I want a ticket, I want a cake.
Yo quiero un boleto.   I want a ticket.
Yo no quiero un...   I do not want (an object) or (an infinitive)
[the word 'no' is pronounced more like the English word 'not' but without the final 't'. I could write it phonetically as 'noh'.

So, the Spanish negative is simple, we just insert 'noh' in front of the verb wherever we would put 'do not'.

I want a ticket.   I **'noh'** want a ticket.
I go to Madrid.   I **'noh'** go to Madrid.

Yo quiero un boleto. Yo **no** quiero un boleto.
Yo quiero ir a Madrid Yo **no** quiero ir a Madrid.

Learn 'Yo' and the following 13 present tense verb-phrases and you are well on your way to finishing your work. (You can abandon using the 'yo' as you progress.) So, let's get down to it.

1 **yo estoy** Pronounced: **yo ess-toy**
Meaning: I am

Some useful words to add on to the present tense 'Yo estoy' meaning 'I am'. For example, the word "can<u>s</u>ado", pronounced **can-<u>sah</u>-doh** means 'tired', which allows you to say:

"Yo ess-<u>toy</u> can-<u>sah</u>-doh"—I am tired.
[Use cansada if you are female and cansado if you are male. Adjectives end in 'o' when describing masculine things and in 'a' when describing feminine things.]

Or, consider the word, "diver<u>t</u>ido", which is pronounced **dee-bear-<u>tee</u>-doh** means 'amused', which allows you to say:

"Yo est<u>oy</u>" divertido—I am amused. *[divertida if you are female]*

The correct use of the two different verbs 'to be' ensures that you are speaking a language fluently, even when you are still working with a limited vocabulary. However, I am sure that if you were to use just 'est<u>ar</u>' for all instances, Spanish people would still understand you. So, I guess you could always use est<u>ar</u>, but, before you speak, think whether the adjective you are about to use is a permanent state of existence (ser) or a temporary one (est<u>ar</u>).

When you are holidaying with your partner and one of you is by the pool, when the other arrives, they can say, "Yo ess-<u>toy</u> a-<u>kee</u>". The word **a-<u>kee</u>** is written 'aquí' in Spanish. So, it is nice, when in Spain and arriving to meet your friend or partner, to say, "Yo estoy aquí", which simply says, in a friendly way, "Hi, I'm here!" Try it.

Digressing a little, you can always use the Spanish word for 'Hi!', which is "¡Hola!", pronounced **<u>oh</u>-lah!** It's nice to have little Spanish words to use, even with your English friend or partner. It will encourage you to feel that you are 'speaking the language'.

Here are a few other words to add on to 'estoy'. If you would like to learn more, then you can look them up in the English part of your small dictionary.

Happy.
(If you are a male), 'contento' pronounced "**con-<u>tent</u>-oh**".
"Yo estoy contento": I am happy.
If you are a woman, 'contenta'
Just learn the right one for you.

Sick, or ill.
In Spanish, 'enfermo' pronounced "**enn-<u>fair</u>-moh**".
"Yo estoy enfermo": I am sick/ill.

The word for 'very' is 'muy', pronounced '**<u>moo</u>-ee**'. So, you can say, for example, "Yo estoy muy enfermo" meaning "I am very sick". *[You may hear Spanish people saying "moy" but don't copy this because it is just a Spanish south-coast accent.]*

---------------------------------oOo-----------------------------

2   **yo tengo**   Pronounced: **yo <u>ten</u>-goh**
                           Meaning: I have (or I possess)

This is also a very useful phrase. Wherever you can think that you use the phrase, "I have" in English, then you can use "tengo".

I have a dog.   Yo tengo un perro.   (**oon per-roh**) With a rr in the middle of a word, try to roll the r. Not too difficult and fun to try. Any r at the beginning of a word should be rolled as well. You don't <u>need</u> to learn these two things, but if you wish to speak more fluently, then practise them.

I have a pain.   Yo tengo un dolor.   (**Yo <u>ten</u>-goh oon doh-<u>lor</u>**)

I have a pain here. Yo tengo un dolor aquí (**a-<u>kee</u>**) 'aquí' means 'here', which is a generally useful word to learn. (Particularly useful if you feel that you need to be clear where your pain is, even if a doctor or paramedic appears to speak English well.)

Or, the following is a very useful phrase using 'tengo'. You do not need a huge vocabulary to explain to a room maid, garage mechanic, or waiter, that you have a problem. If you just tell them that you have a problem and point to it, they will figure out for themselves what your problem is. So, here it is:

Yo tengo un problema.   **yo <u>ten</u>-goh oon prob-<u>lay</u>-mah ak<u>ee</u>**.
                                I   have   a   problem   here.

[Note that the word 'problema' is actually masculine but ends in an 'a'. It is one of a few such anomalies. Another common one is the word for 'water', which is masculine but ends in 'a'. Agua.]

-----------------------------oOo-----------------------------

3   **yo quiero**   Pronounced: **yo kee-<u>air</u>-oh**

Meaning: I want

I believe that this is the most useful phrase you can learn in any foreign holiday language. On holiday it is all about what <u>you</u> want. You have come on holiday to spoil yourself, give yourself treats, eat what you fancy, drink nice drinks, and buy presents and anything else you may see. Hence, the importance of the phrase, "I want". "**yo qui<u>e</u>ro**".

Some useful examples of how to use **yo qui<u>e</u>ro** include:

I want to eat. Yo quiero comer. (**yo qui<u>e</u>ro co<u>mer</u>**)
Note that 'com<u>er</u>' is an infinitive. You will find it in the Prime Verb Table in Chapter 2. Any infinitive can be added after 'I want': e.g. to swim, to drink, to run, to sleep, and so on.
Or 'I want' can be followed by a noun to show that you want an object.

I want a beer. Yo quiero una cerveza
(**yo qui<u>e</u>ro <u>oo</u>na thair-<u>bay</u>-tha**)
[In my phonetics, the letters 'th' are spoken softly as in 'thanks']

I want a newspaper. Yo quiero un peri<u>o</u>dico. (**yo qui<u>e</u>ro oon peh-ree-<u>odd</u>-ee-koh**)

-----------------------------oOo-----------------------------

10   **yo busco**   Pronounced: **yo <u>boos</u>-koh** *[koh as in 'oh']*
                        Meaning: I look for, or I seek

This can be a handy present-tense phrase—especially if you are looking for a doctor. dentist, pharmacy, ironmongers, or any other particular shop. You can look up the name of trade shops in your small dictionary before you go out to ask in the street.

I am looking for a pharmacy. Yo busco una farmacia.
yo boos-koh oo-na far-mah-thee-ah.   *[remember the soft 'th']*

I am looking for a bank. Yo busco un banco.
yo boos-koh uhn ban-koh.

When you are looking for something and asking in public, then it is best to add 'please' at the end of your request:

I am looking for a doctor, please. Yo busco un medico, por favor.
yo boos-koh uhn may-dee-koh por fab-or.

I am looking for my car. Yo busco mi auto.
yo boos-koh mee ow-toh. *[ow is pronounced as in 'now']*

------------------------------oOo------------------------------

13   **yo se**   Pronounced: **yo say**   *['say' as in day]*
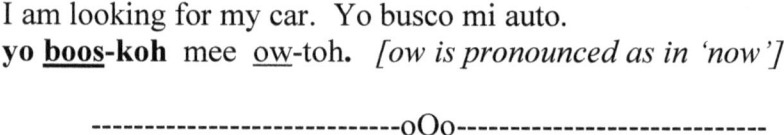

The verb, **saber**, is to know something or some fact. For example, when someone says that you have taken the wrong turn, you can say I know   yo se   **yo say**   or it may be better to use:

I know that or I know it.   I it know   Yo lo sé   **yo loh say**

Your friend says, "By the way did you know that it is raining?" You can reply, **"See, yo say"**. Sí, yo sé. Yes, I know.

While we are on that subject, there are a couple of additional useful responses to people that I can tell you about now. Let's look at them:

I understand.   yo comprendo   **yo com-pren-doh**

Of course, OK, I comply.   por supuesto   **por soo-pwes-toh**

When you want to say that you know about something or have met someone, however, **saber** and the others above are not the ones to use. Nor would it be suitable if you wanted to say that you are familiar with a street name, for example. Then the suitable verb you need is listed in the Prime Verb Table as Number 14 and is cono<u>c</u>er. Pronounced **con-oth-air** *[th as in 'thanks']*

Here are a couple of useful examples:

Perhaps you are looking around for some refreshment, which is when you can say that you know of a café.

I know a good café.   yo conozco un buen café.
yo con-oth-koh uhn boo-en kaf-ay.

I know a beautiful cathedral   yo conozco una hermosa catedral
Yo con-oth-co   oo-na   air-moe-sah   kat-ay-dral

--------------------------------oOo-----------------------------

17   **yo vengo**   Pronounced: **yo ben-goh** *[soft sound 'b']*
                    Meaning: I come, or I am coming

This is handy when your partner says, 'come on!' because you are lagging behind on that fascinating tour of the beautiful cathedral!

You can say, with an assuring tone of voice, **yo b<u>en</u>-goh**—I'm coming!

Or, when the taxi driver looks up impatiently because you are a little late at the hotel door, you can say the same—**yo b<u>en</u>-goh**. But, this time with an apologetic look and a smile. You might add, disculpame **dee-<u>scool</u>-pa-may** as well, in an attempt to mollify him a little. I guess he will expect a minimum 10% tip to appease him.

-----------------------------oOo-----------------------------

18   **yo llego**   Pronounced: **yo <u>yay</u>-goh**
                             Meaning: I arrive

This can also be used in friendly banter when and if you arrive a little late for a restaurant table or a taxi. You can just say **yo <u>yay</u>-goh**, meaning, 'I'm here!'
Then you can add the obligatory, **dee-<u>scool</u>-pa-may!** Pardon me!

The useful application of **yo <u>yay</u>-goh** in the future tense construction is described in Chapter 6. That is where you tell someone when you intend to arrive for your table, or at the hotel, or similar.

-----------------------------oOo-----------------------------

19   **yo voy**   Pronounced: **yo <u>boy</u>**
                           Meaning: I go

This present-tense phrase is also used, primarily, in the construction of the future tense and you will benefit from learning the phrase now because you will need it later.

In its simplest form, you can imagine using it as a small throw-away comment when, for example, you realise that you have been taking far too long to vacate your café table and people are queuing impatiently. You can say, to the waiter, and to the queue, **yo <u>boy</u>** and add **dee-<u>scool</u>-pa-may!** Pardon me! Preferably several times as you hurry away.

---------------------------oOo---------------------------

20   **yo vuelvo**   Pronounced: **yo boo-<u>el</u>-boh** *[soft letter b]*
                    Meaning: I return

This present-tense phrase is also used, primarily, in the construction of the future tense and you need to learn it now because you will need it then.

In its simplest form, you can imagine using it after you have asked the waiter "Where are the toilets, please?"
¿Dónde está el servicio, por favor?
<u>Don</u>-day est-<u>a</u> el sair-<u>beeth</u>-ee-oh, pour fab-<u>or</u>?
When he has pointed them out to you, you might wish to intimate to him that you are not vacating your table permanently, so he shouldn't seat someone else there, and so you can add, "Thank you, I am coming back. I have not finished."
Gracias. Yo vuelvo. No he terminado
<u>gra</u>-thee-as. yo boo-<u>el</u>-boh. No tair-mee-<u>nah</u>-doh.

---------------------------oOo---------------------------

26   **yo puedo**   Pronounced: **yo <u>pway</u>-doh**
                    Meaning: I am able (I can)

Let's say you have tripped up in the street, and have fallen. Concerned people help you up and you want to assure them that you are alright. You might wish to say, I can walk, thank you.

Yo puedo caminar, gracias.
yo p<u>way</u>-doh caminar, g<u>ra</u>-thee-as *[sound th as in thanks]*

This present-tense verb is, perhaps, most useful in its ability for you to ask a question. I find that, on holiday, I am often asking people if I can do something, meaning if I am permitted to do it. For example, I am not sure of whether I can take something, or whether I am permitted to enter a particular door, or exit there, or whether I can seat myself somewhere, and so on. This is where the verb poder can be used to ask 'Yo puedo' as if it were a question. After all, 'Yo puedo' is a statement, but if you raise your voice towards the end, it can become a question without having to change it. Practise it.

Note that, when you are about to speak to a person or to ask a person a question in the street, it is a very good idea to start talking with the equivalent of, "Excuse me, Sir", "Excuse me, Madam", or "Please Sir", or "Please Madam". This gets your voice going which is handy when you may be nervous of speaking, but more importantly, it allows the person a chance to get used to your voice and to realise that you are a foreigner who may not speak Spanish very well. That is most helpful before you launch into your question. So, here are the phonetic phrases to memorise and use at every opportunity.

Excuse me, Sir.
dee-<u>skool</u>-pay-may   sen-y<u>or</u>   Dis<u>cúl</u>peme señ<u>or</u>

Excuse me, Madam.
dee-skool-pay-may sen-yor-ah   Discúlpeme señora

por fa-bor sen-yor   Please, Sir.
por fa-bor sen-yor-ah   Please, Madam.

And afterwards, always:

gra-thee-as sen-yor   Thank you, Sir.
gra-thee-as sen-yor-ah   Thank you, Madam.

And, here are some statements turned into questions by the tone of your voice and the addition of the leading word, 'Please'.

Please,	I can	to exit	here?
por favor,	¿puedo	salir	aquí?
por fa-bor,	**pway-doh**	**sal-eer**	**a-keeh?**

Please,	I can	to sit	here?
por fa-vor,	¿puedo	sentarme	aquí?
por fa-bor,	**pway-doh**	**sen-tar may**	**a-keeh?**

Please,	I can	to pay	here?
por fa-vor,	¿puedo	pagar	aqui?
por fa-bor,	**pway-doh**	**pag-ar**	**a-keeh?**

So, you observe that you can ask just about any question asking if you are able to do something by putting the infinitive of a verb after 'puedo'. You can look up any of the infinitives in our Prime Verb Table in Chapter 2, or, just as an example, if you look up the word 'carry' in a dictionary, it will give you the infinitive, 'to carry' as 'llevar'. You can now ask someone if you are able to carry something by saying:

Please,   I can   to carry   that?

por fa-<u>vor</u>,	¿puedo	llevar	eso?
por fa-<u>bor</u>,	**p<u>way</u>-doh**	**yay-b<u>ar</u>**	**es-oh?**

----------------------------oOo----------------------------

27 **yo veo**   Pronounced: **yo <u>bay</u>-oh**
                      Meaning: I see

I have to confess that, at first sight, this does not seem to be a vital word for you to use on holiday. However, in writing this book, trying to help you to express yourself to Spanish people, I am conscious of the fact that you may well be using the language I teach you to help yourself in emergencies and other difficult situations. Thus, I foresee that your ability to say to someone that you see something may be useful both socially and in the case of difficulty. Here are two examples; the first is social and the second, during a difficulty.

I	see	an	ice cream shop.	
Yo	veo	una	heladería	
Yo	**<u>bay</u>-oh**	**<u>oon</u>-ah**	**el-ah-day-<u>ree</u>-yah**	

I	see	an	accident	there	(while pointing)
Yo	veo	un	accidente	ahí	
Yo	**<u>bay</u>-oh**	**oon**	**ax-ee-<u>dent</u>-ay**	**a-<u>yee</u>**	

----------------------------oOo----------------------------

31 **yo creo**   Pronounced: **yo <u>cray</u>-oh**
                      Meaning: believe (I think that...)

Creer (<u>cray</u>-air) is a useful verb but we use it where the phrase, "I think that I shall..." really means, "I believe that I shall...". It does not mean the usual idea of thinking, in which you are thinking about something—that verb is 'pen<u>sar</u>'. Instead, you use 'cre<u>er</u>' to indicate uncertainty in whatever you say subsequently. It will make your Spanish flow more realistically. For example, in English you might say, "It is going to rain" or "I think it is going to rain". Similarly, you might say to a waiter in a restaurant, "I shall have the soup", or "I think I shall have soup, what kind have you got?" **kay tee-poh eye?** *['eye' as in English 'height or eye']*

You can see that this can be used in so many different scenarios because one is rarely certain about things—especially in a foreign country where customs, habits, and situations can be significantly different from back home. So, here are some examples:

I	think	that	it rains	today.
Yo	creo	que	llueve	hoy
Yo	**cr<u>ay</u>-oh**	**kay**	**y<u>oo</u>-eh-beh**	**oy**

I	think	that	I should	to return	to the	hotel
Yo	creo	que	debería	volver	al	hotel
Yo	**cr<u>ay</u>-oh**	**kay**	**deh-beh-<u>ree</u>-ah**	**bol-bair**	**al**	**oh-<u>tell</u>**

I	think	that	I want	the	chicken.
Yo	creo	que	quiero	el	pollo
Yo	**cr<u>ay</u>-oh**	**kay**	**kee-<u>air</u>-oh**	**el**	**<u>poh</u>-yo**

The first useful phrase is "I think that", which is **Yo cr<u>ay</u>-oh kay**, but also notice the very useful phrase: "yo debería" pronounced **yoh deh-beh-<u>ree</u>-ah**, which means "that I should". It allows you to say lots of things using creer. I think that I should sleep now. I think that I should go now. I think that I should drink water now. I think that I should find the toilets soon. Thousands of things that you might wish to say in a polite way that uses 'I think/believe' at the beginning to suggest that anytime now you will probably need to do something.

There is the alternative possibility that you might wish to use the verb 'pensar' to ask someone to wait a moment while you make a decision. For example, in a shop, the owner might ask you which dress or hat you want to buy. You might wish to ask her to wait a moment while you think. So you could say:

One	minute	please.	I am	thinking.
Un	momento	por favor.	Yo estoy	pensando.
Oon	**moh-<u>men</u>to**	**por fab-<u>or</u>.**	**Yo es-toy**	**pen-sand-oh.**

-----------------------------oOo-----------------------------

32   **yo comprendo**   Pronounced: **yo com-<u>pren</u>-doh**
                                                     Meaning: I understand

And, this last present tense verb is one of the most useful.

You will need to say that you do understand something quite often and that you do not understand something even more often—mostly all the time. So here we go.

Yes,	I	understand.
Sí,	yo	comprendo.
See,	**yo**	**com-<u>pren</u>-doh**

And - <u>more importantly</u>:

No,	I	do not	understand.
No,	Yo	no	comprendo.
No,	**yo**	**no**	**com-<u>pren</u>-doh**

I trust that you have enjoyed learning how to use the present tense to construct verbs that allow you to communicate better with Spanish people when you are on holiday in Spain, South America, Mexico, or other Spanish speaking countries.

The present tense is particularly important because I use it as the foundation for an easy way to create a 'future tense'. The next chapter shows you how.

6 Speak the future tense.

I SHALL ENJOY SPEAKING SPANISH

THE FUTURE TENSE

Simple future sentence constructions

Now that you have learned the present, the Roberts system makes the future very easy to express in most languages including Spanish.

The principle is that, to express a sense of the future, we say the thing we want to say in the present tense and then follow it by what I call a 'future word'. This can be any word or short phrase that indicates a time in the future.

You may not think about it, but that is how we speak English a lot of the time and how, for example, the Spanish, French, and Italians tend to talk about the future when speaking informally.

Before getting into specific examples, let's look at what I mean.

Let's say we are staying in a guest house and the owner enquires when we might be leaving. There are a variety of responses that we could use:

I leave tomorrow. I leave soon. I leave this afternoon. I leave at 1.00 pm. I am not sure when I leave. I leave on Thursday. I leave on the 26th February.

And so on. The list is endless. In this case the verb I used was simply the present tense - "I leave". You can imagine the huge range of future responses we could make by simply adding extra words to the verb.

I realised that all that is needed is a simple list of the present tense verb-words and a list of useful 'future' add-on words.

Let's say that one of your friends asks, "When are you guys going camping?" You may well reply, "Actually, we leave tomorrow morning!" See the present tense? We leave! And so, it is quite common to use the present tense as long as we follow it with what I call a 'future word' or 'future phrase'.

As I have mentioned earlier in the book, I have, initially, selected just 13 out of the 35 possible present tense words found in the Prime Verb Table in Chapter 2. These first 13 are the ones I suggested you learn in order to get going and start talking. Eventually, you would be rewarded by learning all 35 infinitives, past, and present verbs, as well as a good number of add-on words to use for future constructions.

Chapter 8 contains a comprehensive list of suggestions for 'future' words that can be added after the present tense. I'll discuss them generically because, when you wish to use them you will be able to select the exact words you need.

I	pay	tomorrow.	
Yo	pago	mañana.	
Yo	**pa-goh**	**man-yaa-nah.**	*[yaa pronounced as in car]*

Some other similar words are next week, next month, next year, this afternoon, this evening. Or, even more specifically:

I hire a car on the first of January.
Yo alquilo un coche el pri mero de enero
Yo al-kee-loh uhn koh-chay el pree-mair-oh day en-air-oh

You may well be surprised to learn that that is it. We have finished the essential part of the Roberts system for speaking about the future.

But, just to add a little extra useful embellishment, I now mention another couple of ways by which, on holiday, you can indirectly refer to the future.

Implied future constructions

We have finished the essential part of the Roberts system for speaking about the future. But, just to add a little extra useful embellishment, I now mention another couple of ways by which, on holiday, you can refer to the future.

When you use querer to say that you want something or want to do something in the future, than you use the simple phrase you have already learned—**Yo quiero**.

You use this construction with infinitives such as: to go, to eat, to sleep, etc.

yo kee-air-oh eer   I want to go.
                              Yo quiero ir

yo kee-<u>air</u>-oh com-<u>air</u>   I want to eat
                                            Yo quiero comer

yo kee-<u>air</u>-oh dorm-<u>eer</u>   I want to sleep *[pronounce the 'r's]*
                                            Yo quiero dormir

yo kee-<u>air</u>-oh com-air a lass see-<u>et</u>-ay.   I want to eat at 4.00 pm
                                            Yo quiero comer a las cuatro.

What I have done there, is to suggest a kind of 'future phrase' that you can use (a las cuatro) which you can modify as you may need at any time. You can substitute alternatives as you go on. Some of the most useful things you can learn for 'future' purposes are all the numbers up to 31, the days of the week, and the months of the year. That simple exercise will result in your being able to say any future time and date with exactitude, should it be necessary. Those useful dates and times are given in Chapter 8.

These additions may seem onerous at the moment, but their great advantage is that, once learned, they can be applied to any situation to specify a more accurate time in the future. It is also good to know these basics for renting a car, booking a stay at an inn, booking a rail ticket, and the like. You will be surprised that, outside your holiday resort, many people in Spain still do not speak English. That will be a pleasant surprise if you have studied and implemented the contents of our two 'Learn 35 Words/Verbs' books. Not such a pleasant surprise if you haven't.

In the meantime, here are some English examples of typical 'future words' that will be very useful:

This evening, next week, next month, next year, Thursday, Saturday, in two days, et cetera, just to give you the idea.

Another example, twelfth of October   doce de octubre

And so, within our system, to construct a future tense, you need to learn a smattering of handy words to add on to the present tense to construct a sense of the future. There will be just over a dozen new words that you must learn now but many more eventually.

There is also another way of speaking a special, very particular case of the future. This is the case where you are wanting to say that you need to or must do something. So, you use the Spanish words "Yo debo", pronounced **"Yo day-boh"**.

If you want to say that you have to/need to go somewhere or that you have to/need to eat, or sleep, you can say, "Yo debo" plus an infinitive. I provide you with a full list of infinitives in Chapter 5 and you have already learned them.

Examples:

Yo debo +   ir (to go) + mañana: tomorrow.
Yo day-boh   eer   man-ya-nah
I have to/ need to/ or must go tomorrow

Yo debo +   partir (to leave) + más tarde: later.
Yo day-boh   par-teer   mas tar-day: more late
I have to/ need to/ or must leave later.

Yo debo +   comer (to eat) + esta noche: [this evening.]
Yo day-boh   com-air   es-ta notch-ay
I have to/ need to/ or must eat this evening.

You are well on the way to speaking Spanish in the present, past, and future tenses with only the small amount of learning that we have covered above.

While we are talking about easy words to learn, we need to recap these three words.

Yes	Si	Pronounced 'see'.
No	No	Pronounced 'noh'.
Not	No	Pronounced 'noh'.

Using 'si' and 'no' is easy because they just fit in the same as in English.

Here are the previous three sentences made negative.

Yo **no** debo ir mañana.
I do not have to go tomorrow.

Yo **no** debo partir más tarde.
I do not have to leave later.

Yo **no** debo comer esta noche.
I do not have to eat this evening.

And so on and so on. It is wonderful in its simplicity. Using things that you have learned to make complex sentences that convey what you want to say.

It is a little like fitting a jigsaw puzzle together. You recognise and learn all the pieces and then just put them together to make a picture that makes sense—but in our case, we can put the jigsaw pieces together in different positions to make a different picture. It's amazing!

The great thing about my system is that you don't have to learn any future tense at all to be able to speak about the future. You just use the present tense and select any single word or phrase that you might need to use at the time. Then you add it to the present tense and hey-presto, you have a simplified future sentence. Easy.

When you come to Chapter 8, you will see many of those optional words listed, together with their pronunciations. You will not be aiming to learn these before your first or second visit to Spain but you can use that chapter to look up words as they are needed. Eventually, of course, you will need to learn them if you are going to progress with speaking Spanish. You will, ultimately, need to know the days of the week, the names of the months, how to say the years between, say, 2020 and 2030. You will need to know prime numbers from 1 to 31 and ordinal numbers from 1st to 31st. At the earliest stage of your learning, you will certainly need to be able to say prime numbers up to about 12 so that you can order goods in a shop or supermarket up to, say, a dozen eggs.

What exactly, the term 'ultimately' means is entirely dependent upon you. If you just use our book for intermittent Spanish holidays, then you may never actually learn all of these 'future' words. On the other hand, if you develop a great interest in Spanish and don't want to commit to a third or fourth language using our system, then you might learn all of them in the first year following your second holiday in Spain.

That's the fun of it—just see how you get along. The most important thing is that it should be fun. Don't make hard work of it. Enjoy it all.

7 You can speak Spanish.

YOUR DREAM COME TRUE.

You wanted to 'Speak Spanish Better' when you bought this book.

Well now you can!

With just the 35 **words** we taught you in our first series of books, added to the 35 **verbs** you learned here, you can speak an awful lot more and a great deal better. And, you have most likely bought a little dictionary to start learning even more.

Congratulations and well done!

Your knowledge of the local language will not only be useful to you but will represent a source of continual pleasure, increasing your happiness and enjoyment of your holiday.

When you return home from your holiday, you will feel that you have accomplished a great thing. You will have learned and used a foreign language that you did not know before. Not everyone can say that!

It is my opinion that the feeling of achievement is one of our greatest sources of happiness. You will feel proud of your new-found ability to communicate in Spanish and your achievement will make you happy. Well done!

Your friends will certainly be impressed to hear you speaking Spanish on your holiday and your partner will be proud of you.

Finally, let us remind you that our '35' series of books will allow you to learn more than one overseas language. In fact, a second foreign language will be easier to learn than the first. Why? Because each language in our series follows the same system, using essentially the same words, and taking you through the same procedures. Your familiarity with the Roberts rapid learning system will make learning a third and fourth language a breeze! We know that you will enjoy the whole experience, which will change your life for the better.

You won't believe it until you try, but you can now easily express yourself and make the local people smile for an entire holiday. And, if you have bought a small dictionary, you will learn another 35 words and, perhaps, one or two specialist verbs while you are away and you will be well on your way to properly studying Spanish.

Now that you have worked your way through our two Spanish books, you should seriously *consider* going to classes back home and getting a private tutor to keep your Spanish language alive.

That may seem to contradict the words we have said throughout our books—that you should only learn the minimum for a fortnight's holiday overseas. But, our overriding rule is that, before you learn a language, you should sit down and ask yourself seriously why you are considering learning it. In ninety-nine percent of the cases, people will find that our '35 Words and Verbs' approach is perfect for them. But, if you have worked your way through two of our Spanish books, you now need to sit yourself down and have another word with yourself.

Have you enjoyed learning Spanish so much that you would really like to move on and do more? Or, has our '35 Words and Verbs' concept made your realise that you could rapidly learn to speak another holiday language while holding on to the Spanish that you have already learned?

If you want to move on with your Spanish, then you must pose another question to yourself: do you want to expand your Spanish by extending our '35' system by yourself? Making it a '70 Word and 40 Verb' speaking system?

Alternatively, have you fallen in love with Spanish so much that you would find it thoroughly exciting to dedicate two or three years of your life learning it thoroughly—reading, writing, and speaking all the 'verb-persons' and as many of the verbs and tenses as you can stuff into your brain?

It is an exciting prospect, although we know that you will forget most of it subsequently if you are not using it all the time by living in Spain. If you are intending to emigrate and live there, then you **must** go down this route. You cannot live and manage in Spain with just the '35 Words and 35 Verbs' in our books. They are just a launch pad to start you off. You need proper grammatical lessons with lots of good textbooks and a properly-trained teacher. I have mostly had a personal tutor for the languages I have learned and it is money well spent. You cannot learn properly without a personal tutor who should be a professional teacher. If you are going to live in Spain, then get a teacher before you go and get one as soon as you arrive there and keep having lessons!

Finally, and we think this is the most enticing prospect. If you have enjoyed learning our '35' system for Spanish, why not consider doing the same in one of the other European languages that we have covered?

Perhaps you would find it exhilarating to learn holiday German for when you go skiing in the German mountains or Austrian Alps. Or could Italian be your next dream? They also have good ski slopes.

Our system is so minimalist that you will not forget it when you start to learn 35 Words and Verbs of another language. In fact, you can learn and use several holiday languages as you travel around Europe, without a book in your hands.

You will find it wonderful to move across the Pyrenees mountains from Spain into France and simply stop speaking holiday Spanish and start speaking holiday French. Think how great that will make you feel! And think how impressed people will be.

If you are not going to need a career change and you do not fancy committing several years learning Spanish in detail, then do please consider learning another language from our '35 Words' and '35 Verbs' series of small books. It will expand your horizons and take you to even greater levels of holiday enjoyment.

Anyway, here are some of the things that you can now say that you never thought you would.

Some things you can say from our "Learn 35 Words to Speak Spanish" book.

Quiero un café descafeinado.   (dess-caffay-<u>naa</u>do)
I want a decaffeinated coffee.

Quiero té para dos.
I want tea for two.

¿Dónde está la estación, por favor?
Where is the station please?

¿Dónde está el tren para ir a Madrid?
Where is the train to Madrid?

¿Cuánto vale esto? ¿Esta carta? (<u>kwan</u>-toe <u>ba</u>-lay es-toe)
How much is this? This card?

Quiero la cuenta por favor.
I want the bill please.

Quiero un café y dos vasos de limonada, por favor.
I want a coffee and two glasses of lemonade, please.

Disculpe. ¿Dónde está el Hotel Majestic, por favor?
Excuse me. Where is the Majestic hotel, please?

You get on a bus and ask the driver or passengers *'Disculpe. ¿para ir a Madrid?'* (Excuse me. For Madrid?) Simple. They will either nod and mutter *'si'* or say *'no'* and point you in the right direction. We have done this and it really works.

¿Dónde está un taxi, por favor?
Where is a taxi please?

Quiero una cerveza, por favor.
I want a beer, please.

Red wine (*vino tinto*),
pronounced <u>bee</u>-no <u>tin</u>-toe,
or white wine (*vino blanco*),
pronounced <u>bee</u>-no <u>blank</u>-oh.)

Some things you can say from Chapters 2 to 6 in this book.

(I don't expect that you will need the phonetics now that you have worked through the book.)

I want to be happy tonight.
Yo quiero ser feliz esta noche.

I have been to Paris.
He estado en Madrid.

I want to pay now, please.
Yo quiero pagar ahora, por favor.

I want to drink and eat this evening.
Yo quiero beber y comer esta noche.

I want to buy that, please.
Yo quiero comprar eso, por favor.

Is it included?	Is that included? *[point to it]*
¿Está incluido?	¿Eso está incluido?
es-<u>tah</u> een-cloo-<u>ee</u>-doh?	**<u>Ess</u>-oh es-<u>tah</u> een-cloo-<u>ee</u>-doh?**

Some things you can say by adding in words from Chapter 8 of this book.

Here are a few sentences made more sophisticated by adding in extra words that you aspire to learning and using as you take your Spanish language further.

I return to the UK on Monday, first of May.
Yo vuelvo a Reino Unido el lunes uno de mayo.

I think that I go to eat now.
Yo creo que voy a comer ahora.
(Colloquially: "I think that I'll eat now.)

I return next year.
Yo vuelvo el año que viene.
(Colloquially: I'll come back next year.)

I like that. I buy it tomorrow.
Me gusta eso. Lo compro mañana.
(Colloquially: I like this. I'm going to buy it tomorrow.)

I have been into town yesterday.
He estado en la ciudad ayer.

I have drunk a whisky.
He bebido un whisky

I have drunk too much alcohol.
He bebido demasiado alco-ol. (I've had too much alcohol.)

I do not drink alcohol.
Yo no bebo alcohol.

Our closing best wishes.

Don't you think that this is great? You have learned 35 words (plus one or two more sneakily), and you have learned 35 verbs, and you are speaking Spanish much better on your holiday. Well done!

We hope you are as pleased as we were when we wrote these little books for ourselves, on holiday in Spain.

If you do decide that you would like to learn a second or third overseas language, then our "Learn 35 Words to Speak" books are available in a total of eight European languages at present: Spanish, French, Portuguese, Italian, German, Greek, Welsh, and Irish Gaelic.

What makes it easier to learn another language from our series is that they all follow exactly the same procedure using the same verbs.

Consequently, when you learn to speak another language, you immediately feel at home with the books and the system. And, you will have extra confidence based upon your successful experience of learning and using your first foreign language.

But if you don't wish to study this language more deeply and you don't fancy speaking a second or third foreign language, you can always take our two Spanish booklets with you when you go to Spain next time!

With best wishes,

Peter and Helena Roberts.

Happy Holidays in Spain

8   Some Useful Stuff.

FOR YOU.

Here is some useful information that you may wish to dip into from time to time, or more frequently, as you expand your verb and tense knowledge and as your speaking fluency increases.

It is not presented in any particularly logical order.

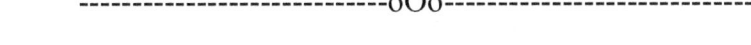

A FEW FUTURE, PAST AND OTHER MISCELANEOUS WORDS AND PHRASES

English	phonetic	Spanish
Tomorrow	**man-ya-na**	mañana
Soon	**en po-co tee-em-poh**	en poco tiempo
Later	**mass tar-day**	más tarde
This evening	**es-tah notch-ay**	esta noche
Next week	**la prox-ee-mah seh-ma-nah**	la próxima semana
Next month	**el prox-ee-moh mess**	el próximo mes
Next year	**el prox-ee-moh ann-yoh**	el próximo año
In two days	**en doss dee-ass**	en dos días

Yesterday	**a-y<u>air</u>**	ayer
Last week	**la-seh-<u>ma</u>-na pass-<u>ah</u>-dah**	la semana pasada
Last month	**el mess pass-<u>ah</u>-doh**	el mes pasado
O.K.	**oh-<u>kay</u>-ee**	OK.
Straight away!	**een-<u>may</u>-dee-at-a-<u>men</u>-tay**	inmediatamente

*[**inmediatamente** can be used in two ways. Firstly, to confirm that you intend to follow an instruction straight away. For example, if a policeman asks you to move your car you can say, "sí, señor, ¡inmediatamente!" Secondly, you can use it to issue an urgent request, say to the room maid, asking for something to be delivered to your room. But, you must add 'Please'. For example, "Quiero un poco de jabón **inmediatamente**, por favor" I want some soap straight away please.]*

[Please note: 'th' is always sounded as in 'thin']

Certainly	**thee-air-ta-ment-eh**	ciertamente
Good morning	**boo-<u>eh</u>-noss <u>dee</u>-ass**	Buenos días
Good afternoon	**boo-<u>eh</u>-nass <u>tar</u>-des**	Buenas tardes
Good evening	**boo-<u>eh</u>-nass notch-es**	Buenas noches
Good night	**boo-<u>eh</u>-nass notch-es**	Buenas noches
Sir	**Sen-y<u>or</u>**	Señor

['yor' as in 'for'. Sound the last 'r']

Madam	**Sen-y<u>or</u>-ah**	Señora
Alcohol	**<u>al</u>-koe-ol**	alcohol
Too much	**deh-mass-ee-<u>ah</u>-doh**	demasiado
Please	**pour fab-<u>or</u>**	por favor
Thank you	**gra-thee-ass**	graçias
Excuse me	**dees-<u>kool</u>-pah-meh**	discúlpame
Excuse me, Sir	**dees-<u>kool</u>-pah meh Sen-y<u>or</u>**	Señor

Is this water drinkable? **es <u>ag</u>-wah poh-<u>taa</u>-bleh?**
es agua potable? *[raise pitch at the end to make a question]*
Is this free of charge? **<u>es</u>-toe es grah-<u>tees</u>?** ¿Esto-es gratis?
[point to the object]

---------------------------oOo---------------------------

CARDINAL NUMBERS

Remember, phonetic 'th' is always pronounced softly as in 'thin'

	Phonetic	Spanish
1	**<u>oo</u>-noh**	uno
2	**doss**	dos
3	**tress**	tres
4	**<u>kwah</u>-troh**	cuatro
5	**<u>theen</u>-koh**	cinco
6	**<u>say</u>-ees**	seis
7	**see-<u>et</u>-ay**	siete
8	**<u>otch</u>-oh**	ocho
9	**noo-<u>eh</u>-bay**	nueve
10	**dee-<u>eth</u>**	diez
11	**<u>on</u>-thay**	once
12	**<u>doh</u>-thay**	doce
13	**<u>treh</u>-thay**	trece
14	**kat-<u>or</u>-thay**	catorce
15	**<u>keen</u>-thay**	quince
16	**dee-eth-ee-<u>say</u>-ees**	dieciseis
17	**dee-eth-ee-see-<u>et</u>-ay**	diecisiete
18	**dee-eth-ee-<u>otch</u>-oh**	dieciocho
19	**dee-eth-ee- noo-<u>eh</u>-bay**	diecinueve
20	**bay-<u>een</u>-tay**	veinte

21	bay-**een**-tee-**oo**-noh	veintiuno
22	bay-**een**-tee-**doss**	veintidós
23	bay-**een**-tee-**tress**	veintitrés
24	bay-**een**-tee-**kwah**-troh	veinticuatro
25	bay-**een**-tee-**theen**-coh	veinticinco
26	bay-**een**-tee-**say**-ees	veintiséis
27	bay-**een**-tee-see-et-ay	veintisiete
28	bay-**een**-tee-**otch**-oh	veintiocho
29	bay-**een**-tee- noo-**eh**-bay	veintinueve
30	tray-**een**-tah	treinta
31	tray-**een**-tah ee **oon**-oh	treinta y uno

-----------------------------oOo-----------------------------

ORDINAL NUMBERS

	Phonetic	Spanish
1st	pree-**may**-ro	primero
2nd	seg-**oon**-doh	segundo
3rd	ter-**ther**-oh	tercero
4th	**kwar**-toh	cuarto
5th	**keen**-toh	quintoh
6th	**sex**-toh	sexto
7th	**sept**-ee-moh	séptimo
8th	oct-**a**-boh	octavo
9th	noh-**bay**-noh	noveno
10th	**day**-thee-moh	décimo
11th	oon-**day**-thee-moh	undécimo
12th	doo-oh- **day**-thee-moh	duodécimo
13th	day-thee-moh--ter-**ther**-oh	decimotercero
14th	day-thee-moh--**kwar**-toh	decimocuarto
15th	day-thee-moh--**keen**-toh	decimoquinto
16th	day-thee-moh--**sex**-toh	decimosexto

17th	day-thee-moh--**sept**-ee-moh	decimoséptimo
18th	day-thee-moh--oct-**a**-boh	decimoctavo
19th	day-thee-moh--no-**bay**-noh	decimonoveno
20th	bee-**hay**-see-moh	vigésimo
21st	bee-**hay**-see-moh pree-**may**-roh	vigésimo primero
22nd	bee-**hay**-see-moh seg-**oon**-doh	vigésimo segundo
23rd	bee-**hay**-see-moh ter-**ther**-oh	vigésimo tercero
24th	bee-**hay**-see-moh **kwar**-toh	vigésimo cuarto
25th	bee-**hay**-see-moh **keen**-toh	vigésimo quinto
26th	bee-**hay**-see-moh **sex**-toh	vigésimo sexto
27th	bee-**hay**-see-moh **sept**-ee-moh	vigésimo séptimo
28th	bee-**hay**-see-moh oct-**a**-boh	vigésimo octavo
29th	bee-**hay**-see-moh noh-**bay**-noh	vigésimo noveno
30th	tree-**hay**-see-moh	trigésimo
31st	tree-**hay**-see-moh pree-**may**-roh	trigésimo primero

MONTHS OF THE YEAR

[Note: Spanish months do not start with a capital letter.]

January	**en-er-roh**	enero
February	**feb-rair-oh**	febrero
March	**marth-oh**	marzo
April	**ab-reel**	abril
May	**ma-yoh**	mayo
June	**hoo-nee-oh**	junio
July	**hoo-lee-oh**	julio
August	**ag-os-toh**	agosto
September	**sept-ee-emb-ray**	septiembre
October	**oct-oob-ray**	octubre
November	**noh-bee-emb-ray**	noviembre
December	**dee-thee-emb-ray**	diciembre

DATES OF THE MONTH

You need to know a little more than these lists if you are going to talk about days of the month or dates. In connection with days of the month, the Spanish just use the cardinal numbers with two exceptions—the 1st and 2nd of each month, when they use the ordinal numbers. To assist with clarity, the following are examples which you can check against the cardinal and ordinal listings above.

the first of May	el primero de mayo (ordinal)
the second of May	el segundo de mayo (ordinal)
the third of May	el tres de mayo (cardinal)

All subsequent dates are spoken as cardinal numbers.

DAYS OF THE WEEK

Monday	**loon-ess**	Written: lunes
Tuesday	**mar-tess**	Written: martes
Wednesday	**mee-air-coh-less**	Written: miércoles
Thursday	**hoo-ay-bess**	Written: jueves
Friday	**bee-air-ness**	Written: viernes
Saturday	**sa-ba-doh**	Written: sábado
Sunday	**doh-meen-goh**	Written: domingo

CURRENT YEARS

You may well need to say the year sometimes, and so I thought it, perhaps, useful to just tell you how to say some typical years. Later, you will need to be able to read and write these as you progress with your studies. Perhaps, learning 2021 to 2025 would be handy and a good start.

Number	Phonetic	Spanish
1900	**meel <u>no</u>-bay-thee-<u>en</u>-toss** mil novecientos	
1995	**meel <u>no</u>-bay-thee-<u>en</u>-toss no-<u>ben</u>-tah ee <u>theen</u>-koh** mil novecientos noventa y cinco	
1999	**meel <u>no</u>-bay-thee-<u>en</u>-toss no-<u>ben</u>-tah ee noo-<u>eh</u>-bay** mil novecientos noventa y nueve	
2000	**doss <u>meel</u>** dos mil	
2020	**doss <u>meel</u> bay-<u>een</u>-tay** dos mil veinte	
2021	**doss <u>meel</u> bay-een-tay-<u>oon</u>-oh** dos mil veintiuno	
2022	**doss <u>meel</u> bay-een-tay-<u>doss</u>** dos mil veintidós	
2025	**doss <u>meel</u> bay-een-tay-<u>theen</u>-koh** dos mil veinticinco	

2030   **doss meel   tray-een-tah**
        dos   mil   treinta

Of course, when you are writing the year as a number, it is just the same in Spanish as it is in English. 2021 is 2021.

THE TIME

To speak the hours of the day, you have two options depending on your circumstances. The first is to use the continental 24-hour clock. The second is to use the a.m./p.m. notation.

The 24 hour clock is spoken by using the cardinal numbers of 1 to 24 plus the numbers of minutes, followed by the words 'hora' pronounced '**or-a**' or 'horas' pronounced '**or-ass**'.

Thus:
Three in the morning: 0300 hrs.
tress or-ass   tres horas

Seven thirty hours   0730 hrs.
see-et-ay tray-een-tah or-ass   siete treinta horas

We say 'half-past seven' and they say 'seven and half'.
see-et-ay ee may-dee-a   siete y media
                                 [media means a half]

Sixteen hundred hours, 1600 hrs. which is 4.00 in the afternoon.
meel   say-ees-thee-ent-ass   or-ass
mil   seiscientas   horas

Four twenty-five in the afternoon   4.25 p.m.
kwat-roh   bay-een-tee-theen-coh   de   la   tar-deh
cuatro   veinticinco   de   la   tarde

**For booking lunch, here are three useful times.
12.45 p.m., 1.00 p.m., and 1.15 p.m.**

12.45 pm   **doh-thay   kwah-rent-a   theen-koh**
                   Doce   cuarenta   cinco

1.00 pm   **la   oo-na   en   poon-toh**
Or use   la   una   en   punto
1300 hours   **meel   trays-thee-ent-ass   or-ass**
                   mil   trescientas   horas

1.15 pm   **oo-na   or-a   keen-thay**
Or use   una   hora   quince
1315 hours   **tray-thay   keen-thay   or-ass**   *[th as in think]*
                   trece   quince   horas

And, the following is pretty well all you need to say in the restaurant to book your table, with the addition of 'please', as always.

I want to   reserve   a   table   for   two   at   one
kee-air-oh   ray-zair-bar   oo-na   may-sa   pa-ra   doss   a   la   oo-na
Quiero reservar una mesa para dos a la una

-----------------------------oOo-----------------------------

www.ingramcontent.com/pod-product-compliance
Lightning Source LLC
Chambersburg PA
CBHW070936160426
43193CB00011B/1709